Jamil Qureshi is one of the UK's foremost practitioners of performance-enhancing psychology, hypnotherapy and neuro-linguistic programming. He works with a host of celebrity sports people, as well as global businesses, and was the official psychological performance coach for the European Ryder Cup team. He regularly appears on television and is in constant demand in the media.

www.jamilqureshi.com

D1421441

700039301269

THE MIND COACH

BE THE PERSON YOU REALLY WANT TO BE

Jamil Qureshi

Vermilion
LONDON

5 7 9 10 8 6 4

Published in 2008 by Vermilion, an imprint of Ebury Publishing

Ebury Publishing is a Random House Group company

Copyright © Jamil Qureshi 2008

Jamil Qureshi has asserted his right to be identified as the author of this Work in accordance with the Copyright, Designs and Patents Act 1988.

The Random House Group Limited Reg. No. 954009

Addresses for companies within the Random House Group can be found at www.rbooks.co.uk

A CIP catalogue record for this book is available from the British Library

Mixed Sources
Product group from well-managed
forests and other controlled sources
www.fsc.org Cert no. TT-COC-2139
© 1996 Forest Stewardship Council
FSC

The Random House Group Limited supports The Forest Stewardship Council (FSC), the leading international forest certification organisation. All our titles that are printed on Greenpeace approved FSC certified paper carry the FSC logo. Our paper procurement policy can be found at www.rbooks.co.uk/environment

Printed and bound in the UK by
CPI Mackays, Chatham ME5 8TD

ISBN 9780091923570

Copies are available at special rates for bulk orders. Contact the sales development team on 020 7840 8487 or visit www.booksforpromotions.co.uk for more information.

To buy books by your favourite authors and register for offers, visit www.rbooks.co.uk

The information in this book is general in nature and not intended to constitute nor be relied on for professional advice. The author and publishers disclaim, as far as the law allows, any liability arising directly or indirectly from the use or misuse of the information contained in this book.

This book is a work of non-fiction. The names of people in the case studies have been changed solely to protect the privacy of others.

To Tammy, who has taught me everything I know about living a better life. Without her love, support and belief I would never be who I am now.

Contents

Acknowledgements

I would like to thank my parents and brother for love and support way beyond what was deserved.

A huge thank you to Julia Kellaway, whose skills as an editor are only surpassed by her patience with deadlines.

Immense gratitude to Malcolm Mortimer, whose help with this book and years of friendship have been so valuable … Jules, your endurance is admirable.

Thanks to Andrew 'Chubby' Chandler of *International Sport Management* for help, guidance and always the best advice. A calm head and a sharp mind, Chubby has all that I admire in those who run a great business. I look forward to his continued success.

Thank you to James Devane and William Dewsall for the start in my early business life. One for his capacious knowledge, organisational skills and brilliant looks of derision; the other for his exceptional business acumen, which comes wrapped up in an energy and enthusiasm that cannot be matched.

I am delighted that Rowan Lawton at the William Morris Agency is in charge when it comes to all things to do with books.

Thank you to Melf Soennichsen and Till Pohlmann at HUGO BOSS; a company that truly understands the meaning of quality and customer service.

... And to every talented individual with whom I have had the privilege to work.

Introduction

I HAVE THE good fortune and pleasure to work with some of the most successful people on the planet. One thing I've realised is that everyone can improve in some way. You don't need to learn new skills to improve. It's simply about understanding what you do, and then doing it a bit better.

Working with professionals from diverse fields – from Premiership footballers to fighter pilots, from CEOs to celebrities – I've found that the route to improvement is based on our perception of ourselves and the world around us. All of us are talented enough – but we perform only as well as we allow ourselves to. The key to performing better is to remove the inhibitors that get in the way.

I have spent four years putting together the ideas in this book – the principles of Mind Shaping. The techniques and ideas are not only useful but also easy to understand and use immediately.

Why Does Mind Shaping Work so Well?

Within these pages you'll find all you need to help you succeed in life. You'll discover how to achieve success at work, in your social life and in relationships. What's more, my Mind Shaping techniques have been designed to make it all as easy and painless as possible.

I'm going to begin with a bit of a negative statement:

'Most self-help books and programmes don't work very well.'

Why should Mind Shaping be any different? And why don't most of these other techniques work as well as they should? The fact is that most 'life-changing' programmes want us to *stop* doing something altogether (like smoking) all at once. Or *start* doing something (like a diet) – again, all at once. These represent major changes to what we are doing now. Inevitably, these changes put us under a huge amount of pressure. Change has a nasty habit of doing that because it rips us out of our comfort zones without so much as a 'by your leave'. Doing things this way also generates unrealistic expectations: if you initiate a major change in your lifestyle, you expect to see rapid results – it's only human nature. Worse, your friends and colleagues – from whom you find your new regime hard to conceal – also expect to see quick results. You become only too aware of this, and the pressure mounts …

Quite simply, you are making life hard for yourself. Most of us seem to have grown up with a belief in all sorts of masochistic aphorisms such as, 'No pain, no gain' and 'If it tastes horrible, it'll be doing you good.' While there might well be an element of truth in such dictums, there's no rule that says you *have* to do things the hard way, particularly when there might be an easier option!

Where Mind Shaping differs from most other self-help programmes is that I advocate making just a tiny change at a time in a very small aspect of your life – what I call the *'one degree change'*.

Imagine standing at the start of a stretch of railway track with two parallel rails running off to a distant horizon. Then imagine what would happen if you were able to unbolt one of the rails and set it just one degree away from parallel. The difference would be barely noticeable from where you're standing now but, 50 miles down the track, those rails (I am assured by my friendly local mathematician) would be nearly a mile apart!

Broadly following Dr James Lovelock's Gaia hypothesis, it is often suggested that a butterfly flapping its wings somewhere in South America could – through all manner of knock-on climatic effects – influence the weather patterns of Western Europe. Tiny variations really can generate significant change. Tiny variations aren't going to cause you that much pain. Tiny variations are realistically achievable. And tiny variations aren't going to put you in the spotlight of expectation.

My belief is that you should let people around you notice the results of your 'one degree change' gradually, almost as if the results have crept up on them over time. This is a more effective approach than looking for improvements every day, and being disappointed and disillusioned in the apparent absence of dramatic progress. That's when people start believing that 'such and such a programme doesn't work' and they stop trying.

Another real benefit of gradual change is that it is easier to incorporate into your lifestyle on a solid, long-term basis. If change is slowly growing in your daily life – like a climbing plant weaving through a trellis – it is much more likely to become an integral part of everything you do. Wholesale change that is imposed dramatically is many times more likely to be unstable and thus reversible.

Remember, the essence of this book is making self-improvement as easy as possible. Just as the best way to eat an elephant is 'one chunk at a time', the best way to change your life is 'one degree at a time'.

How to Make the Best Use of this Book

I've always been puzzled by our attitude towards books. From a very young age, we are taught to revere books, to handle them gently, to turn a page by carefully locating the tip of a corner to eliminate any risk of creasing or tearing. Furthermore, we have been brainwashed into believing that we have to read a book from the beginning to the end, preferably a chapter at a time. Books, in my house, used to be treated almost as works of art to be displayed on shelves and handled with kid gloves. But I want you to forget these notions when it comes to *The Mind Coach*!

This book is to be treated as a tool. When you come across a phrase, sentence or paragraph that really says something important to you, highlight it. Underline sections and scribble big circles round any sentence or paragraph that takes your fancy. Add your own notes. Fold over corners of important pages or even tear them out. Don't worry if it looks used and well-thumbed … it should! That's the idea. After all, you don't panic if a spanner gets a bit oily, do you? You simply wipe it clean and make sure that its usefulness as a tool remains unimpaired.

I also urge you to dip into the book in a random fashion. Sure, there is a notional order in which it has been written, but my intention is that you should be able to scan any page and read something interesting and relevant. I want you to feel that you can dip in when you're relaxed or angry, and feel better for having found something new or enlightening.

This book is the tool with which you are going to tweak, tune and improve your life. Make it work for you in whatever way it can be useful (even if that use is propping up a table leg). But please, make sure that it's your own copy, and not one belonging to the public library!

CHAPTER 1

Learning from Life

LIFE IS ONE long learning opportunity. Many of us fail to appreciate that we can learn – and grow as individuals – from everything that happens to us, both good and bad. Indeed, the more prepared we are to learn, the less likely it is that things will simply 'happen' to us, and we become able to exert a greater influence over life's outcomes. So harnessing and understanding our power to learn puts us where we really want to be … in control.

To be able to learn, however, we need to identify learning opportunities when they arise. Sometimes this demands real creativity. What seems, at first glance, like a complete disaster can sometimes be turned on its head to reveal an opportunity. Perhaps, for example, you know someone who lost their job and, forced to re-evaluate their life, went on to learn new skills and become even happier in a new profession. Or it may just be that you need to look at the possibilities a little more carefully – a bit like studying an optical illusion in a book – to reveal the learning potential of a life situation.

This aim of this chapter is twofold:

1. To help you spot learning opportunities (believe me, they are all around us – often in the most unlikely places).
2. To help you exploit them.

Do this successfully, and you'll be well on the way to making yourself a better all-round person, coping with whatever the world throws at you, and living an infinitely more satisfying life.

What Will You Learn Today?

This is a very simple technique deployed by some of the most successful people I have ever worked with. At the start of the day ask yourself two questions, and keep them in mind:

1. What will I learn today?
2. What will I enjoy about today?

Do this for a week. There is no need for any great analysis. The exercise will force you to consider each event or incident that happens to you in terms of its effect on your life, rather than just letting things drift past in a sort of non-specific haze. You will be putting everything into a sharper focus. All the individual components that, together, comprise your 'average' day will be much more meaningful. You will learn that there is no such thing as a 'bad day': a day might contain one or two bad moments, but they don't have to taint the entire 24 hours!

As you begin to appreciate that everything you do or experience has its own unique value, it will make you much more aware. As simple as asking yourself these two questions sounds, by doing so you will enrich every single minute of your life. By breaking your day down into individual events, you will instantly begin to acquire a better understanding of what life is about.

The more important question of the two is: 'What will I learn today?' This is because the lessons you learn from life today can have an immediate, positive effect on what happens tomorrow. However, the fact is that you learn better when you are enjoying yourself. So by consciously identifying – and seeking – enjoyable moments, you will actually start to feel better about life, and thus better able to learn from it.

Everyday Learning Opportunities

The postman delivers the mail in which there is a credit card bill. You know it will be a big one, and are dreading opening it. In fact, you've been dreading its arrival for days

– your financial situation is not too clever, and it's been hanging over your life like a cloud. Sure, you can afford the payment – just – but this time, don't just rush it through your personal admin system and forget about it. After all, the same worry will be clouding your happiness in another month unless you confront it properly. This time, consider it carefully, with all its implications. Make the decision to tackle your financial issues and do something about them, using the detailed information that bill provides. Once you begin to deal with a problem, you are halfway towards solving it. It really is the old 'divide and conquer' strategy: if you allow worries to gang up and immerse you in one vast, vaguely defined pool of slime, they'll seem insurmountable. But if you isolate them and start to pick them off, one by one, they'll diminish far more rapidly than you might think. Today's big bill can help you *learn to face up to your issues* – not just the financial ones, but all of them.

You get the kids washed, dressed, breakfasted and ready for school. Today, value the time you're spending with them. Don't let it all flash by in a hurried, short-tempered dash to meet departure deadlines. Consciously smile and have fun with them – appreciate the moment. They will certainly remember it as being pleasantly different, and you will launch the day on a high, rather than being stressed from the outset. *Learn to value time spent with your nearest and dearest*, partly because it's enjoyable, and partly because you never know how long you will have them for.

Next, you're driving to work and, as always, there are idiots on the road in a tearing hurry – rude, inconsiderate drivers liable to upset your smooth journey. This time, try and accept the inevitable with good grace. Smile at people, let them into the traffic, thank them when they do something good. There might only be one of you, but your bright, cheery attitude can give many others around you a lift. You will find, too, that you will drive better than when you are cross and irritable and you will arrive at work in a far more positive frame of mind. *Learn to be a more patient and tolerant driver.*

At work, your boss asks you to add yet another task to your already overflowing workload. In the past, you might have taken it on board with a long sigh and resigned yourself to more long hours. You might have worried about how on earth you were going to fit it all in. You might even have doubted your own ability, assuming that the request was probably quite reasonable but that you were just a slow worker. All in all you would have allowed a low level, background resentment to build up – a sense of unfairness – without tackling the root cause. This time, question the request politely but firmly. Make it absolutely clear that you are happy to do as much as you possibly can in the time allotted, but that if the task is too big it might overrun into another day. Stand your ground without being in any way confrontational. If this causes difficulty with your boss, be aware that it is your boss's problem and not yours! Once you have made your point, loud and clear, it is out in the open. It makes it far less easy for your boss to take you for granted – or exploit your good nature – in future. It might well be that such 'exploitation' in the past has not been deliberate. There are many things that don't even register as blips on people's radars until someone actively points them out. Making your point reasonably and fairly shouldn't automatically rock any boats. By confronting the cause of your resentment (however low level that might be), you will feel lots better. *Learn to be more assertive!*

When you're out for a walk in your lunch break, make eye contact, smile and say 'Hello' to someone you pass in the street. Acknowledge or compliment someone you wouldn't normally. Surprised (because we don't tend to do these things much any more), that person might light up the moment with their own smile and greeting. Result? You feel good! You feel a genuine surge of positive energy when something like this happens. Your world becomes a friendlier, warmer place when you choose to interact with other human beings, rather than just exist in your own little universe. *Learn to be more sociable!*

You make your weekly visit to the gym. You've been on the treadmill and decide to give the cross-trainer a good go, but after five minutes your calf and thigh muscles feel hot and wobbly. This time, don't give up! Set yourself a sensible, realistic target and stick with it – all it takes is a bit more self-discipline. Start as you mean to go on and the results will speak for themselves. Okay, it might seem a bit much like hard work, but what's another two minutes? *Learn to go the extra mile.* Work out what it is that allows you to perform better. What went through your mind that enabled you to do that extra two minutes? And, more importantly, what were your feelings at the time? How did they allow you to achieve that goal?

GRAHAM'S STORY

'Dear Graham

'I suspect that this will be the letter you hoped you would not have to receive ...'

The day had dawned – as any other – without any special fears, apprehensions or expectations for Graham Gallagher, his wife Suzy and teenage son Rory. The couple worked from home, running a moderately successful business as foreign language translators. Shortly after midday, Graham left his desk and went downstairs to the kitchen for some coffee. Turning as he heard the slap of the letterbox flap, he saw three or four ordinary-looking letters tumble on to the front door mat. Having filled the kettle he returned to collect the letters, which he briefly scanned. One – addressed to him and bearing an 'NHS Hospitals' franking stamp – attracted his curiosity.

He was used to receiving letters from the hospital: one confirming his annual appointment for what he referred to as his 'MOT' – a regular visit to the heart specialist to check the state of his damaged valves. And another, a few weeks later, telling him that the x-rays and echocardiogram results showed no dramatic changes – 'see you in another year's time'.

With a twinge of apprehension, he opened the envelope, unfolded the letter and began to read it in the softening light of autumn sunshine. Unusually it was from the senior consultant himself. As he completed the first sentence, a chill ran through his veins – partly of disbelief, partly of inevitability. Quickly he became aware that his mind was racing, and it was with a mixture of fear, curiosity and even a bizarre sense of thrill that he read on.

> **'Following the results of the tests that we conducted during your recent visit to the hospital, the team has discussed your case in detail. We now feel that the time has come to seriously consider remedial surgery for your heart valves.**
>
> **'I appreciate that this will come as something of a shock to you, and invite you and your wife to come and see me as soon as possible in my consulting rooms to discuss your situation ...'**

Graham went into 'autopilot'. He wandered back upstairs to his office with the coffee. He sat, gazing absent-mindedly out of the window, as life carried on normally in the road outside the house. Eventually he got up and took the letter through to his wife's office. He felt vaguely detached from reality and, even faced with an upheaval to family life as serious as this, still enjoyed that perverse sense of satisfaction you get from being the first bearer of breaking news.

It was also at this early stage that he began to try and identify any 'positives' that might be presented by this new situation. He was a great believer in the idea that experience was wasted if you couldn't learn at least something useful from it. Melodramatically, perhaps, he tried to imagine how his grandfather must have felt as he stumbled through the nightmare of the Great War's Passchendaele battlefields. How – although he would never talk about the truly awful moments – he seemed to emerge from his experiences a stronger, wiser, more thoughtful and more tolerant man. Maybe this was Graham's moment to face the reality of mortality head-on and, hopefully, to win through and emerge a better, more rounded person. Of course, his new situation was infinitely less horrific than his grandfather's but, to him and his family, the possibility of death was every bit as real. Even though friends kept trying to cheer him up by telling him that it was 'a routine operation nowadays', it wasn't them going under the knife …

A slightly unreal meeting with the consultant ensued a few days later, with Graham soon realising that his options were limited. No, there was no mistaking the readings from the echocardiogram. No, there was no possibility of a mix-up with another patient's tests. Graham's choice was 'die within five years from heart failure', or have two valves replaced – ASAP – while he was still relatively fit and healthy. Graham and Suzy both knew what had to be done.

Once out of the meeting, Graham dwelt briefly on the 'unfairness' of what had happened some 18 years earlier. He had contracted a severe heart infection which all but killed him, and left him with considerable damage to his heart valves. He was immediately advised of a 'probable' need for replacement valves before he was 60. Back then, as he was only 32 when it happened, this seemed a lifetime away. And anyway, 'probable' didn't mean 'definite', so maybe open-heart surgery wasn't inevitable …

The shocking letter he hoped he would never have to receive – he was only 50, after all, and pretty much free of any symptoms – jolted him back into reality. It seemed that the latest thinking advised valve replacement 'sooner rather than later', to avoid irreversible damage to the heart. The die was cast. Once he had accepted that there was no escaping the situation, Graham became quite detached from what was happening and began looking at it as a project that had to be managed and completed … with a profit at the end.

Curiously, although not religious, he came to realise that he had no special fear of death. His single worst nightmare, however, was the possibility that a botched operation might render him a permanent invalid. He worried about that – about the pressures it would place on those around him – and made a conscious decision to invest total belief in the capabilities of his surgeon and nursing staff, and would allow no one to suggest otherwise.

He also made some quiet preparations 'just in case', completing the near-impossible task of composing a letter to his wife and son, to be delivered only if he never pulled through. He put financial arrangements in order, and generally readied everyone for a 'seamless handover', if necessary. He also began to create, in his mind, another world that he called 'the bubble' in which, for maybe three weeks, he was prepared to live another life. He likened it to going away on a training course, during which he would experience many things he had never previously encountered. And from which he would try his damnedest to learn something about himself and others.

When the day came for his admission to hospital, Graham was ready to shut himself away in this 'other world'. Although a natural worrier, he vowed to let his family get on with their lives and make decisions as if he simply wasn't there. But first he had to face the painful task of saying goodbye to Suzy, shutting her out of the bubble. When the moment came, late in the afternoon, both were aware that this might be the last time they would speak to each other. Once she had left the ward, however, he began to get really stuck in to the realities of hospital life, to take his mind off the next day's big operation.

He reasoned that he had absolutely nothing to lose – and much to gain – by making life in the bubble as happy, fun and positive as it could ever reasonably be. He quickly appreciated that this meant being unafraid of making a fool of himself. It meant talking to strangers, joking, smiling and listening. Often, without realising it, he was supporting and encouraging his fellow patients. To Graham's astonishment, the ward in which he was 'imprisoned' quickly became a wonderfully sociable, friendly and supportive environment.

It was one of the last wards in the country not to have bedside television, and even the traditional radio system was broken. So the only 'entertainment' came from a motley selection of human beings sharing a common interest in their own survival and recovery. Here – with everyone much closer to the live rail than was comfortable for them – he experienced true 'gallows humour'. He passed an evening of hysterical hilarity with three diverse and stimulating characters. Two had just undergone major heart surgery; the other had just had a cancerous lung removed.

Talking – and listening – to perfect strangers became an exhilarating and uplifting experience for everyone. Then there were the visitors. Graham had never really appreciated their importance before. Whenever anyone he knew had been in hospital in the past, he was reluctant to visit. Some friends he expected to see at his bedside were the same, and he understood all their reasons, such as genuine fear of hospitals and being too busy. One – with brutal and refreshing honesty

– owned up to having a 100-per-cent fatality record for people he'd visited in this particular hospital! What really surprised Graham, though, were the people who did turn up, many of whom he'd never considered likely candidates at all. These immediately became more special friends, as did those who took the trouble to telephone. They would share part of his life-changing experience the others could never be a part of.

Setbacks were another challenge to be met. There were several – some pretty serious – but Graham coped fine, strengthened by the discipline of the 'bubble'. He accepted and worked through these local difficulties and was deemed ready for discharge – as he had prayed he would be – after 10 long days.

Notification that he might be released came as a surprise. It depended upon his lying on the bed quietly, hooked up to a cardiac monitor. Various readings had to be consistently safe for 60 everlasting minutes. He lay there, trying to remain calm, listening to favourite music on his MP3 player. As he did so, wave upon wave of sheer relief engulfed him: every track threatened to release – embarrassingly – the tears of joy brimming in his eyes, so he kept on changing his selections. It was like the end of a film with a fabulous soundtrack, and he was the star. He felt himself almost looking down from the white, tiled ceiling, viewing his body spread-eagled on the bed, attached by a matrix of wires to a futuristic machine that was constantly bleeping and tracing his heart rhythms on-screen. This was it – soon he would be free from the bubble. In his emotionally charged state, it seemed almost like a rebirth.

Graham passed the tests and returned home that afternoon. It was probably the most concentrated and positive learning experience he had ever undergone. It put workaday life into crystal-clear perspective, and highlighted to him life's most valuable asset: his interaction with other people.

Graham's Experience

Graham, like we all are sometimes, was suddenly faced with circumstances completely outside any previous personal experience. Sure, he had seen things like this on television but this time it was up to him to provide a script – at least for his character.

Put yourself in his shoes. First he had to face up, once again, to the apparent 'unfairness' of the original random heart infection. For nearly 20 years he had managed – ostrich-like – to bury his head in the sand, live 99 per cent normally and forget the weight hanging over him. Then, having virtually convinced himself that – as treatments improved – the operation might never be needed at all, BANG! 'That letter' exploded on to his doormat.

Secondly, fair or not, he had to face the reality of a major operation. However commonplace, it still involved his ribcage being sawn apart and prised open, and his heart being physically 'unplugged' from his body and repaired on some bench like a car's water pump! Then there was the fear of infection, which could prove so far out of anyone's control that he daren't even consider it.

He needed a coping strategy, and what worked for him was seeing the whole thing as a learning exercise, albeit one devised by some particularly demanding teacher.

Although Graham made the conscious decision that he would approach this event by taking this approach, we all sometimes – without knowing – develop coping strategies.

Maybe you can think now of a time when life's circumstances demanded something of you, and you dealt with it brilliantly. What was your coping strategy? What was the framework or mindset in which you made your decisions and navigated your way through it? Can you remember how you felt and how you created an internal climate for good decision making?

Maybe like Graham you went one step further than merely trusting in fate or God: he decided that he would be proactive and positive. He would not simply try to get through it all intact; he would actually benefit from it. It was that challenge that helped him cope, and took his mind off the unpleasant reality he would face for the several weeks until he made a full physical recovery.

In addition to recognising the operation as a potential learning opportunity, Graham also – without realising it – created an ideal environment in which to learn. If he were a plant, going into his 'bubble' would have been like re-potting himself in a specially fertilised bed with brilliant soil, great drainage, perfect temperature control and just the right amounts of water and sun. He had no excuses not to grow and develop as a person.

By seeing this as a learning opportunity he found it easier to detach from the predicament he found himself in. It was easier for him to remain cheerful and optimistic, which not only made him feel and respond better, but also lifted those around him. Everyone benefited, even the complete strangers visiting his fellow patients, and the medical staff who treated and looked after him.

Think about Success

Think about some people you perceive as successful (don't forget that there are many ways to measure success). I want you to think about their background. You may be aware of some of the incidents and accidents in their life, but one thing you start to realise is that they come from very different backgrounds. It really does go to prove that life is all about how you choose to play the cards you are dealt. Your ability to learn and grow is more important than wishing or hoping for constant 'good luck'.

Turn Failure into Feedback

We tend to perceive our actions as either failures or successes. This is one reason why you may not see life as the learning opportunity it is. As soon as we see things as a failure, we take it personally. The learning opportunity gets lost in the fog of self-doubt and bad feeling. However, being turned down, rejected or refused doesn't mean you're inept, incapable or bad. It simply gives you feedback on how to do it better next time.

In fact, there is no such thing as failure, just feedback.

Have a think about some of the things you would label as successes and failures in your life. It doesn't have to be a long list (hopefully the list of successes will be longer!) for you to realise that what you label as success or failure is personal to you – other people may label things differently.

You may find it helps to have a reference point for your view of success. This doesn't have to be a detailed picture, but when you see yourself at some stage in the future as successful, what does it look like? You may have a picture of yourself sitting on that fabulous beach, or spending three days a week off with the children in some wonderful house in the country.

Whenever you experience a 'failure', bring to mind your view of yourself being successful. How might this recent setback actually contribute to you being closer to where you wish to be? What did you learn that will take you nearer reaching your goal? This may require some imagination, as the 'failure' may seem like a terrible blow, taking you further away from your goal. However, opportunity often comes from adversity; we just need to find it.

Take Time Out to Think about Your Life so Far

Take five minutes out every week to sit down quietly and ask yourself: 'What did I learn (about myself) from my last three relationships?' The following week, ask yourself what you learnt from your last three jobs, and so on. When you look back at the incidents and events of your life, do you do so with emotion, replaying them simply to relive how they made you feel? For example, do you cringe at the memory of forgetting your lines in that presentation, or fume at the way you didn't say what you should have done to the boss? Conversely, do you have the learning mindset when you return to those past events, asking yourself how you could have done it better? What would have got a different result? Next time what would you change?

Thinking about how you could have reacted better to situations will help you devise a strategy for coping with future events. Try and look at each obstacle you face – regardless of how unfair it might seem – as a challenge from which you can learn something. Then let yourself learn. The more you do this, the more you gain control of your life, and the easier it becomes to tackle the next problem down the line.

Points to Remember

- **Bad things happen. Most will contain an opportunity to learn, but it's up to you to try and find it!** Don't just panic – look at your new situation and consider everything carefully.

- **Exploiting the learning opportunity will help you cope with the crisis** – and grow as an individual when it blows over. Opportunity and hardship are often one and the same.

- **Don't be scared of making a fool of yourself in order to learn from life.** Babies try and walk – unsuccessfully – for weeks or months before succeeding. They don't care that they look silly. It doesn't bother them that they keep falling down – they just keep on trying until they learn what they set out to achieve. You can learn from them!

- **Successful people in life are not necessarily those blessed with the greatest talents or the most privileged backgrounds.** They are those who have the wisdom and flexibility to be able to react to trials, tribulations and disasters in the most appropriate fashion. Being willing to try and learn from the random challenges of life is a tremendous way of coping, of becoming a better person and of helping those around you to do likewise.

- **Success is not about making fewer mistakes.** It's simply about our ability to learn, develop and grow from the mistakes we do make.

CHAPTER 2

Real Life is Now!

To MAKE LIFE better for ourselves in the future, it's absolutely vital that we are genuinely aware of what we are and what's really going on around us ... right now! And if you think that you are aware, think again, because most of us aren't.

The aim of this chapter is:

- To help you see your world with greater clarity and do away with the bias that interferes with the facts.

How We See the World

You see, the world isn't how it is – it's how we are. If two people are presented with the same evidence, they will probably see it differently. For example, you and a friend are having a drink in a bar. A stranger talks to you both for five minutes then leaves. You discuss the stranger with your friend and find that you have different views on them. This is despite the fact that you were both presented with the same evidence: the words you heard and clothes you saw, and so on, were the same for both of you. Your different views on the same evidence must, therefore, come from your individual interpretation. You will delete, distort and filter information according to your own belief system, using 'values' that have developed from all your past experiences.

Being truly aware means being able to look at life as it happens, as if seeing it reflected in a flawless mirror. Life that is not distorted in any way by any value judgements we might make. The trouble is, we're not very good at accepting the present for what it really is. **We all make judgements** about what is happening to us now, rather than living the moment with an uncluttered mind.

Making Value Judgements

We judge things as being 'good' or 'bad', rather than simply as neutral. As soon as we label things like this it makes us look at them in a distorted way. Imagine you quite fancy someone, but you find yourself thinking, 'I wish he (or she) was six inches taller because all my exes were tall.' Every time you're in their company, that little voice keeps distorting your view of this height-lacking person. Think how different things could be if you were simply to take them exactly as they are, warts and all. You either fancy so-and-so, full stop, or you move on until you find someone you like who meets your altitude qualifications. Life becomes so much clearer and more relaxed when you don't add all the complications of being judgemental.

LIVING IN THE PAST AND IN THE FUTURE

We seem to base these judgements either on our past experiences or on a sort of in-built wish list. In fact, **we seem to live perpetually either in the past or in the future**. So instead of appreciating what we are actually experiencing *now*, we find ourselves looking back and mentally comparing life with things that have already happened. 'This is like that night at so-and-so's birthday bash when Janet and I split up,' or 'If I have another drink, I'm bound to make an idiot of myself.'

We also tend to get ahead of ourselves, either daydreaming or assuming the worst: 'Wouldn't it be great if they decide to offer me that job?' or 'I know what's going to happen – they'll think I'm too old.' Even if you're lying on a beach on holiday, do you find yourself thinking about what you'll be doing that night and what you did the previous evening, instead of just enjoying that beach moment? Haven't we all been guilty of feeling unhappy two days before the holiday ends just because we know it's nearly gone?

The trouble is that making judgements of either type distorts the present and **is likely to affect our future**. So tomorrow ends up like a twisted stroll through a fairground hall of mirrors! What on earth is the point of living in the past or future when it is what you do now – in the present – that determines the immediate course of your life? React to events in your life as they really are, not as you would prefer, imagine or guess them to be.

You Can't Predict the Future

We are not very good at predicting what will actually happen in the future. We tend to go ahead, merrily making judgements based on past experience that determine how we behave today. This behaviour, in turn, will influence what is going to happen in the future. But the judgements we make are, inevitably, seriously flawed because nobody knows what surprises – what twists and turns – the future has in store for us!

In 1974 Dr Schulman, from the University of Minnesota, came up with an amazing psychological discovery. He established that people are particularly bad at determining how happy or sad certain events will make them. Over a period of six years he researched people who had lost limbs in accidents, and people who had won substantial amounts of money. He found that both sets of people grossly misjudged their forecasts of how they would feel in years to come as a result of the event.

We're not great at handling the past, either. Despite what we often seem to think, the effects of what has happened in the past need never be permanent. Your past does not equal your future. Patterns are never inevitable – accidents do not have to happen in threes. They can be modified by what you do right now. And what you do right now can exert a huge influence on what will happen in the future.

It's too easy to fall into the trap of judging situations to be 'identical' to ones that have occurred before. Of course, they might be quite like them – even very like them – but they are never identical. The mere fact that time has elapsed counts for something. And even if the people involved happen to be the same, time and experience will have changed them. Whether or not you realise it, you will have changed, too! Nothing stays the same, so there is no good reason to think that outcomes will be exactly the same in the future as they were in the past.

Remember, if you go for that job interview, the seat you sit on won't care whether you get the job or not, nor will the carpet or the weather that day – even if they do remind you of that last interview where you didn't perform well.

Learning to Live in the Present

When you are depressed – I mean clinically depressed, rather than just generally fed up – it is often impossible to appreciate the reality of a situation. What tends to happen is that you see everything in terms of 'wishing you could change the past', or anticipating the future. In fact, often you become completely obsessed with the past and future at the expense of the present. So what you are doing is stopping yourself from being able to exert any control over your life.

I know this sounds obvious, but it's worth saying as we frequently act as though we have forgotten it: you can never go back and change what has already happened. You can 'edit' it in the present – perhaps correct some aspects of it – but you can't go back to square one and start all over again. Neither can you predict with certainty what will happen in the future (except that you'll pay your taxes and, eventually, pass through that final checkout). The only time you can do something to change what you are experiencing now ... is now.

There really is no earthly point in assuming that something will happen in the future, and basing your immediate behaviour and attitudes on worst-case scenarios. I know a man who spent weeks and weeks in a sort of limbo – not getting on with his life at all – because he faced a life-threatening operation. Unlike Graham in the previous chapter, all he seemed to be able to think about was a) what if he died? and b) what if he lived but suffered problems that turned him into a cabbage? He spent ages worrying about how to prepare the family finances to cope with these possibilities. He almost totally overlooked the most likely option – that he'd survive and be cured. So he wasted a significant chunk of his all-too-short life somewhere in a hypothetical future, when he should have been actively living it! You can't live tomorrow, today – except in the pages of a science-fiction novel. And the only way you can take control of your life is by looking at the situation that actually exists, and dealing with it minute by minute.

Not everything that happens in our lives goes exactly

according to plan. Take the friend of mine whose wife decided to leave him, completely out of the blue. Not only did she leave, but she moved overseas to live with her sister, and took their daughter with her too. This, naturally, was devastating to Alec, but he appeared to be getting over it gradually. After a couple of years, he began a relationship with a woman at work and seemed a changed man. The spring returned to his step, and they got engaged to be married. However, there were skeletons in her cupboard that she hadn't properly dealt with, and Alec had really only papered over the cracks of his marriage break-up. So it wasn't exactly a relationship based on the firmest of foundations.

Things began to go wrong. She had second thoughts, and he became desperate not to let another major relationship disintegrate. I wondered whether she was in the right mental state to be doing this. I knew that he wasn't. Together they were almost bound to implode, and I pointed out this possibility to Alec. Although he agreed, he still couldn't stop himself. It all became very fraught and unworkable, and he eventually decided to make a clean break.

Perhaps a little hastily, he applied for a new job hundreds of miles away. He got it, and all seemed wonderful for a few weeks. However, he soon discovered that people in charge of his working environment were decidedly 'dodgy'. He uncovered suggestions that illegalities were going on and being covered up. Indeed, they even tried to pressure him into becoming an accomplice: the entire set-up was rotten. This meant that Alec now saw his professional life, as well as his private life, as a disaster. He couldn't go back to his old job because his former fiancée was still there, and seeing her every day would destroy him. And he desperately missed his young daughter. Sadly, under this immense pressure, he spiralled deeper and deeper into depression.

He would call me regularly on the phone, and came to stay several times. For months, all that he would talk about was the past. He came to believe that his wife had left because of his behaviour (something he had never even considered before). Why had he not seen that he was becoming antisocial and boring? If only he had seen that, then she would not have left with their daughter. It was all his fault. And why had he fallen so deeply for that stupid woman at work? She had forced him away and broken his heart. But why had he trusted the people in his new job, and not seen that the set-up was so dodgy? Why was he such a fool with such poor judgement?

This was, quite literally, all that we talked about, time and time again. Round and round and round and round and round we went. Tears flowed. Apathy ruled. He hated himself, no matter what his friends said or did to boost his confidence. He became physically ill.

But one day – after 18 months or so of abject misery – he found a way out of the maze. He finally decided that he had to deal with the present. He began to accept that, yes – maybe he had taken his eye off the ball in his marriage and got into a rut. So be it. That was desperately unfortunate, but it was done. End of a chapter in his life. Book closed. But there was something that he could do now – today – to brighten up his prospects for the future. He could re-establish proper contact with his daughter, which he managed to do quite quickly.

Then there was that woman. He began to see that what I had suggested about her might actually have been right. That it might *not* have been all his fault, and that it might have been destined for disaster whatever he had done differently. All this he began to accept as he started to see reality for what it was and not through a fuzzy, distorted lens. He also realised that he had no logical reason to doubt that he had made a sound decision in taking his new job. Anyone would have jumped at it. It wasn't his fault, either, that the powers that be were dodgy. It was simply bad luck. No amount of 'if onlys' could have changed anything.

All of these things became clearer and clearer as time went on. Alec found himself another – much better – job, and really did start to live in the present. He shared holidays with his daughter and managed to get on well as a friend with his ex-wife. Ironically, he had only one real regret: he wished he had been able to appreciate and accept 'now' for what it was then. That he had been able to see what was real, and what he could do at the right time to make the best of it. Had he been able to do that, he would never have hit the rocks as spectacularly as he did.

So what can you take from this? As I said before, there is no point in doing anything other than living for the moment. Of course, you will make various contingency plans for the future, such as set up a pension and make a will – all the boring, sensible things we should probably do. But not at the expense of living life to the full as it happens, rather than in a slow-motion replay. Doing that is a bit like forever being behind the lens of the home DVD camera at all the big family events, and never enjoying them for what they actually are. I've done that plenty of times and it really does get pretty boring!

Be Open Minded

All we have is the here-and-now, with no associations to past failures. That's logical. But since when did logic have anything to do with how human beings behave! Still, this isn't rocket science, and the answer is a whole lot easier to find than you might think. All you have to do is let the logic work for you. And the way to do this is by allowing yourself to be open minded.

Being open minded in this sense means allowing surprises to happen, rather than assuming that everything will follow the same old pattern. They do happen – they are a part of real life. We don't expect them to happen, but then that's what makes them surprises. And surprises can change everything.

I recently met an out-of-work teacher who was so far down on his luck that, at 54, he thought life was all but over. Still, he gave himself one last crack at a job interview. To his amazement, he got it. He was going to an Arab state to teach physics at an international school. Within a week of his arrival the headteacher had packed it all in, his deputy had taken over, and our man found himself being asked to take on the deputy headship of the school! Life-changing things do happen.

Try to start appreciating the moment for what it is – living right now is so much easier than forever living with regrets or crossing bridges before we get to them. Remember, **it is within your power to make outcomes different**. And it really isn't that hard to do. Just live in the moment. Don't judge it. Develop awareness. Allow yourself to be open minded and – little by little – you'll open the door to positive change.

THE STORY OF MIKE AND ROY

Have you ever been captivated by an overheard conversation on a bus or a train? A few years ago, I was in just such a position on a train bound for London from Nottingham. It was a bitterly cold, dismal and grey afternoon. The two men seated at the table across the aisle from me clearly knew each other – quite possibly, their conversation hinted, from university days. Clearly, too, both appeared slightly ill at ease. It was decidedly warm and stuffy in the carriage, and the more talkative of the pair – Mike – seemed rather stifled and uncomfortable in his respectable dark grey suit. The second man – Roy – was dressed in a tweed jacket, rugby shirt, jeans and scarf. To me, he also looked uncomfortable in his clothes, and that he would have been happier in a suit. Perhaps they should have swapped, I thought to myself.

The two men were gradually discovering what had happened to each other over the past few years. Mike, it seemed, had followed an interest in broadcasting, inspired by experience in local radio when at university. However, it sounded as though he had been banging his head against a brick wall trying to get something more long term than freelance work. He had attended huge numbers of interviews with the BBC, from which he had received 'enough rejection letters to wallpaper our smallest room' and was decidedly bitter about his application record. He was travelling to another one – in Luton – that afternoon, and it seemed that all he expected to get from the experience was his expenses! The BBC, he railed, were 'boring, completely bereft of imagination and just like a branch of the bloody civil service'. He didn't seem to need much encouragement to vent his spleen. What a great mindset for an interview! Roy, meanwhile, nodded in all the right places.

The train crossed a swollen river, and Mike was now in full spate. He'd been to one radio station – 'Northampton, Nuneaton ... can't remember' – where he'd applied for the role of rock show presenter. One of John Peel's old producers – up from London to sit on the panel – had asked him for ideas on the future of the show, given that listening figures were dropping away. Delighted to get a question that he'd really thought about beforehand, Mike had launched into what sounded like a thoroughly sensible and pretty creative solution. As the 'opposition' station's own rock show was too good to compete against, they should axe the present format and concentrate on something slightly different. I was riveted. Then, just when things were getting interesting ...

'Tickets, please, gentlemen. Thank you kindly.'

As I handed over my own ticket for clipping, the train began to reduce speed. Shortly afterwards we pulled into a station. As the train eased away again, the activity in the carriage slowly settled. Roy, I noticed, was just finishing a call. He smiled slightly quizzically as he tucked his phone into his inside pocket then suggested to Mike that they share a taxi at Luton. Apparently Roy was supposed to have been on holiday until the next day, but someone at his work had called in sick. 'They asked me if I'd mind standing in at some meeting.' This news seemed to perk Mike up, despite the fact that the punch line to his rock show story was, once again, a trifle bitter. He hadn't been selected but, three months later, the show had indeed been axed, just as he'd advised.

With a sympathetic smile and shrug of his shoulders, Roy turned round to the snack trolley we had all heard chinking up the carriage. He bought two coffees. I reflected on how negative Mike was being. Surely it took two to tango! But Roy? He was something of an enigma. He'd not given much away at all, and I couldn't really work him out.

At last, Mike stopped bemoaning his relationship – or lack of it – with the BBC, and I began to discover a little more about the more reticent man across the carriage. Mike recalled that Roy had been something of a high-flier in the law department, and was aware that he had secured an impressive-sounding position as a company lawyer somewhere 'up north' – Newcastle rang a vague bell. When I heard him rather enviously assume that a big career promotion would explain why Roy was now working down south, the disarmingly honest and some-what sheepish reply surprised me. This was not the case, as Roy had apparently suffered 'a bit of a breakdown'. The news clearly took the wind out of Mike's sails, and he seemed embarrassed. 'Oh, I am sorry, mate – I didn't know.'

Following a spot of 'garden leave', he had seemingly drifted into another career, one he rather vaguely described as 'a bit of a civil service-type thing, really'. Hadn't I heard the civil service mentioned earlier in the conversation? Mike seemed to be trying hard not to probe over-zealously, but clearly wanted to know almost as much as I did.

Now more animated, Roy confided that his new role was a lot less stressful, and was 'okay', but still steered clear of much detail. Mike commented on how unlikely it was that they should both end up in Luton, of all places, on a bleak winter's afternoon. Roy just seemed pleased to have re-established an old contact, and to have enjoyed hearing Mike recount his recent past, however negative it sounded. I had to agree that Mike did have the knack of painting pictures with words which, as Roy observed, would serve him well in radio, should he ever make his breakthrough. Indeed, he seemed genuinely supportive as he advised Mike just to keep on knocking at the door, as 'you never know what's around the next bend – I'll vouch for that!'

Mike seemed appreciative, but nevertheless relapsed again. Pleasingly, though, this time it sounded more like black humour than bitterness as he recalled an interview he once had for the television programme *That's Life*. I remembered the programme well, a curious mix of consumer action and downright silliness. People used to send in vegetables shaped like genitals, and play tunes on brass bedsteads. Mike had applied and been called for an interview – down to the last 20 out of 5,000 for two places on the team, he said. But it had been a 'fix', he reckoned, as a couple of the other applicants seemed like old friends to the receptionist. Mike seemed resigned to the fact that the interview that afternoon would follow a similar path.

By now, as I felt once again the gentle judder of the brake, I was pretty sure what was round the next bend for me ... Luton station. But for Mike? I had a weird feeling about him, just from something Roy had said about his new civil service-type career. He never elaborated at all. Was he being wonderfully discreet for Mike's benefit, or was I being too clever by half, putting two and two together and making five?

As the train eased into Luton, I felt I really knew this pair. I wanted to bid them farewell, but that would have been a bit of a giveaway. As they finalised their plans to share the taxi, Mike enquired about Roy's meeting: was it anything exciting? 'Not really – just sitting in on some recruitment interviews ...'

Surely not, I thought. Things like that just don't happen in real life ... do they?

Mike's Experience

We've all overheard similar tales of woe. Mike is living in the past. Travelling to attend a job interview, he has clearly become somewhat embittered by previous rejections. Unfortunately, his negative past experiences are going to determine his mindset for that day's interview. He isn't remaining open minded at all – in fact, he's being a bit of an idiot, thinking he knows what 'they' are going to be like and will be thinking. He appears not to consider the possibility that they might not fit the stereotype he has created in his mind. The danger is that his demeanour and attitude in the interview will actually push the board into the very behaviour patterns he dislikes and resents so much.

Can you think of a time when you may have done this? Have you ever been so certain that someone is a particular way that you've made them become it? We've all heard someone say, 'I'll be nice to him when he's nice to me,' which is a perfect example of behaviour reflecting back.

Remember, Mike has no actual knowledge of exactly who will be interviewing him – right now he is simply guessing and making assumptions about the near future, based on ignorance. He is so 'in the past' that he completely fails to be aware of what is happening in the present. He isn't listening all that closely to what Roy is saying.

If only he would stay absolutely in the present, he would not be pre-judging the upcoming interview – he would simply be looking forward to the unknown. Not necessarily with undue optimism, but certainly not with pessimism. He would be ready to treat every moment on its immediate merits, and be prepared to be surprised. By adopting this attitude, his mind would be sufficiently flexible to be able to react to reality, and to identify positives if and when they decide to show themselves.

From what Mike was saying on that train, we could all picture the likely development of his interview – well, at least *his* end of it – without ever seeing it. He would go into the radio station with a defensive attitude. He would, in a bizarre way, assume that the board already knew of his past 'failings' (as he saw them), and would behave as if they were judging him. But what he obviously wouldn't know is that – through a quirk of fate – Roy would be on the interviewing board. Furthermore, he would see past Mike's negativity and, in all probability, rescue him from making any irretrievable blunders. Indeed he would, quite probably, help him get the job. Who knows?

Remember: only if you allow yourself to be open minded and non-judgemental, and can live life right now, can you hope to appreciate – and benefit from – surprising situations.

Creative Problem Solving

Think of a current problem or challenge.

Now think of impossible solutions.

Now I really mean impossible. Be as inventive as you can. Do it until you smile, and then until you laugh.

For example, the problem is you need more money. Imagine that you win the lottery. Imagine you get a pay rise because you wore the right shoes on Monday. Imagine that you woke up and could speak Chinese, making you more skilled and therefore getting that bonus. Imagine that the cat decided to get a part-time job!

Continue to think of the problem and really enjoy all the crazy solutions you come up with. You don't have to be sitting with your eyes closed doing this; if you're pushing the Hoover round, that's fine. Just make sure you have some fun and, importantly, that you notice how you feel when you think of your silly solutions.

After you've had some fun with this, start to think more practically. Instead of the cat getting the part-time job, could you get another? Instead of waking up speaking Chinese, could you get more skilled?

As you begin to think sensibly, continue to keep those light, relaxed feelings you captured when you thought 'outside the box'. Allow yourself to be surprised that, by exercising your creativity and relaxing, you can come up with some interesting new ways of looking at things. Remember, this isn't a paper exercise; it's a chance to get crazy with ideas in your head.

Have you ever come up with a great idea or the answer to a problem while relaxing in the bath or watching television? You see, sometimes just being in a different state of mind allows us to see with greater clarity. Those brilliant ideas don't need to be forced out of us; they can just rise to the surface.

This is a really useful exercise in being open minded. It also allows you to see a problem with different 'pictures' attached to it. The only real way you can change the way you feel is to change the pictures in your head and the words you use.

Remember to stay in the present, be open minded and creative. Like everything, this takes practise. You'll find that the more you do this exercise the more fun it becomes, and the better you get at finding real, practical courses of action.

I Spend Half my Life Worrying about Things, Half of Which Will Never Happen

Write a quick list of things that you have done that turned out well, but where the decision was delayed or compromised in some way because you wrongly predicted the outcome.

You will notice a couple of things. Firstly, you are not Derren Brown and cannot predict the future. Secondly, our view of the outcome, in most cases, is not wrong because we are inaccurate with the facts, but because our interpretation of our own or others' behaviours and thoughts is inaccurate. For example:

- You buy a flat for investment purposes, the market conditions worsen and you lose money: you got the facts wrong.
- You don't buy a flat because you believe that whenever you invest it goes wrong and you will not be able to afford the mortgage payments if at some stage you lose your job. You believe that making money through being entrepreneurial isn't for people like you: your judgement is wrong.

You may wish to keep two different-coloured pens to hand when at your desk – one for fact and one for interpretation. When you find yourself thinking in terms of fact, write down a couple of examples (it may just be part of your 'To Do' list anyway). For example:

- Finish presentation for 2.00pm
- Call boss and organise weekly review
- Make 20 sales calls by end of day

All of the above examples are fact, but if you catch yourself coming out with any non-facts during the day (make sure you really look for them) write them down in a different colour. For example:

- I hate presenting at the sales meetings because everyone else is so confident
- Everyone hates getting sales calls
- I never make good phone calls after lunch
- I won't write the report as I won't do it as well as someone else
- Nobody listens to me anyway
- It's not my role to get involved in that
- I haven't got enough experience to come up with suggestions yet

Get used to what they look like so you can identify them and eradicate their influence over your decision making.

Points to Remember

- **You will only ever see things with clarity if you are non-judgemental.** Things are neither 'good' nor 'bad'; they just are. History has given us many examples of people who have achieved greatness from what some may say is adversity. However, maybe to them it was opportunity.

- **Sometimes judging others is a reflection of how we judge ourselves.** If you think about what you don't like in other people, it is sometimes what you don't like in yourself. Remember, it doesn't mean you have that trait, you may just think you have. We must be open minded and accepting of ourselves before we can be so of other people.

- **If you are imagining the worst scenario, take time to vividly imagine the best!** We all have a powerful imagination so why use it simply to conjure up negative situations? Go wild imagining even the most impossible good fortune – you will be surprised how it makes you feel.

- **Enjoy a few conversations this week with someone you know where you lose any sense of history.** Try not to look at them as a product of their experiences, measuring them by what they have and haven't done, and by what's happened to them. Allow yourself to be immersed in a conversation or meeting which is simply based upon that moment. Likewise, even with a stranger, enjoy that 'now' moment without prejudice.

- **Understand that wherever you are now is exactly where you should be.** We spend a lot of time worrying about what we haven't got, and what we haven't done. This is usually done in comparison to other people, but success can only be measured against our own potential – what we are personally capable of. The fact that you are bothering to read this book says you are different. Without judging your past, simply allow yourself to understand that you can start to see your world differently. This alone will lead to you making different decisions, trust me.

CHAPTER 3

Banish Indecision

As I HOPE you realise by now, this book is dedicated to helping you improve your life. Let's face it – you wouldn't have picked it up unless you thought it might be able to help you in some way. You've probably already identified some aspect of your life that could be improved. It might be that you'd like a job with more money, satisfaction or, ideally, both! You might be fed up with being on your own and feel that meeting a new partner would liven things up. You might want to sort out a longstanding relationship problem of some sort – a family feud, perhaps. Or get healthier, move house, or any of an endless list of possibilities.

Whatever your reason, you need to do *something* – to be proactive rather than just let life happen to you. By doing something, you'll be in control of your own destiny. Positive thinking is not enough. In fact, any thinking is not enough! Success is the result of action. You will find more opportunities by 'doing', not by waiting. Life will never be truly satisfying if indecision and apathy are blocking your path forwards.

Even when people realise that there are aspects of their lives that can be improved, they often don't do anything about it. For a whole raft of reasons, they procrastinate. You'll say to yourself that you don't want to rock any boats; that you might find it too hard; that other people might not react in the way you want them to.

But everyone is capable of good decisions – you have already made many. You also don't need all the facts or any assistance. You only need to have an understanding of your own process with regards to giving yourself the best opportunity to make the right choices.

How to Make Good Choices

If you are faced with a choice, which one do you opt for? Do you say, 'Oh, I can't decide – I'll put it off until tomorrow'? Don't worry – it's absolutely normal to procrastinate. It's not illegal yet, and I bet you don't know one single person who hasn't indulged!

However, most people's destructive procrastination comes from believing that out of, say, the two choices they've got, one will be right and the other will be wrong. You might be able to think now of something you remain undecided upon. Are you unable to make a decision because you believe one will be woefully unsuccessful and the other just fabulous?

FACT: You'll never be able to take control of your life if you keep putting off the decision to do something about it. It seems so obvious, I know, but it has to be stressed. The truth is, there often is no 'right' or 'wrong' option. As long as we fully commit to whatever decision we make, it will be better than doing nothing at all. And only when we fully commit can we achieve real focus and purpose. This is the fuel for success for each and every one of us, the fuel that gives us the power to make it all work.

Remember, a small change is all it takes to start the process of change. As long as you commit to it, things will begin to happen. Often, too, a small move on one apparently insignificant day can set off a snowball effect before you know where you are.

DARREN'S STORY

The K Club, County Kildare – just 40 minutes from Dublin – was, in 2006, the venue for golf's Ryder Cup, one of the greatest events in the world's sporting calendar. The Ryder Cup is a biennial battle for supremacy between the best golfing men that Europe and the USA can pit against each other.

The night before the first day of the tournament, a violent storm lashed the magnificent golfing grounds. Yet by 8 o'clock in the morning, the tail end of Hurricane Gordon had blown itself out. Thanks to the work of a fantastic supporting cast of groundsmen and green-keepers, the K Club was ready for the Ryder Cup.

The emotional storm that had raged through the recent life of golfer Darren Clarke had caused personal damage on no less a scale. The bulwark of the European team, the Ulsterman's world had been turned on its head by the terminal illness of his wife, Heather. Tragically, if mercifully, Heather's four-year battle with cancer ended less than two months before the Ryder Cup 2006 was due to start.

Imagine yourself, if you can, in Darren's shoes, emotionally exhausted following the battles he and his wife had fought against a common enemy – cancer. Perhaps all you'd want to do would be to hide yourself away from the hurly-burly of life, lick your wounds and hope time would be the great healer that everyone always assumes. After all, you would be emotionally bruised and battered beyond belief, wouldn't you? Or maybe you'd see that as giving up. Maybe you would prefer to 'get straight back on the horse' and let everyday life fill the void in your soul, and not allow yourself to sit there churning over all the inevitable but useless 'if onlys'? Because you wouldn't be able to change anything and at some point, however you reacted, you'd simply have to get on with the business of living life again.

I know what I'd want to do but I have no idea – until faced with such a decision – whether I would be strong enough to take the positive option. Remarkably, by 8 o'clock on the morning of Friday 22 September, Darren Clarke – almost supernaturally calm and focused – was ready for anything.

'I had no other choice,' he said.

In the immediate aftermath of his personal tragedy, Darren's participation in the team was in doubt. Captain Ian Woosnam and his vice-captain, Peter Baker, were desperate: 'He's our talisman, the heart-beat of Team Europe. We need Darren with us at the K Club.' They called him, supported him, urged him, cajoled him. A massively influential personality – a true and proven winner on every golfing stage – Clarke was eventually persuaded to play.

That dark night in September, from the warmth of his hotel bed, Darren heard the gale roaring outside and the rain lashing against the window pane. Was he ready? He had played only once since Heather's death – in Madrid, a week earlier. Not so much for the golf, but to try and release some of the inevitable pressure generated by the world's press. It had gone pretty well, all things considered. But tomorrow? Tomorrow would be a whole different ball game. Could he cope when all those thoughts came flooding back? Would the weight of expectation be too much? Would he be overwhelmed by the unbelievable emotional support he was getting – not just from his European colleagues but from the Irish crowds and even his American opponents?

'This is simply something that must be done. There's no turning back. I'll find the strength from somewhere. I'll have to.'

There *was* no way back now. The ball was rolling. Not just for the golf tomorrow, but for the rest of his life. The future was unstoppable. 'I've got to make the best of it.'

He knew, too, that when he set out on that long walk to the first tee, his head would be totally scrambled, but that he had to trust completely in his ability to focus on each critical moment. He placed himself in the hands of providence, and drifted into a fitful, adrenalin-fuelled sleep.

The day dawned fresh, bright and breezy, the storm now many

miles east of the K Club. Darren's match was due to start at 8.40am. Shortly after 8.30, encouraged massively by his great friend and partner for the day, Lee Westwood, he set out on that momentous walk from the locker room he had imagined the night before. As anticipated, the crowd was amazing, every single one of them wishing him well with an empathy and intensity he found quite staggering. How could you let these people down in your wildest dreams? His head was an emotional soup. Almost automatically, in step with his great friend, he moved on towards the tee, acknowledging this terrifying support with nervous smiles and sporadic, safety-valve fist-pumps.

The reality of the glory that is life hit him with all the force of Hurricane Gordon as he made his way on to the green. A frenzied crowd of around 3,000 people, incredibly close and banked high in temporary seating to the rear and sides of the teeing ground, bayed in anticipation as he came into view: 'Clarkey, Clarkey, Clarkey!' Some 6,000 feet stamped their thunderous, spine-tingling appreciation.

As if all that wasn't enough, the warmth of the welcome he received from US captain Tom Lehman and players Phil Mickelson and Chris DiMarco would have melted the coldest of hearts. Darren smiled, breathed as deep as he dared, and desperately gritted his teeth.

'On the tee, representing Europe, Darren Clarke.'

The reedy, renowned voice of Scots starter Ivor Robson announced that the time had finally come. The world held its collective breath. A million people tried to put themselves into Clarke's Dry-Joy golf shoes. Both Americans were nervous and had tried to play safe but, despite their caution, neither had found 'Position A'. Darren seemed not to notice what his opponents had – or had not

– done. In spite of the mayhem going on around him and, moments earlier, in his own head, he was able to concentrate on constructing an almost visible cocoon of focus. If ever he was to trust in his ability to triumph over adversity, it had to start now. He would be positive, and trust in all the gods that he could summon to help him hit the ball hard and long. Were he able to hear it, the silence would have deafened him.

As he bent over and placed his ball nervously on the high golf tee, it wobbled slightly but, reassuringly, remained in place. One huge, lung-filling, head-clearing breath, one brief practice swing – and then one utterly instinctive, totally committed, immensely powerful swing through the ball. Exploding off the face of Darren's driver, it took off steeply and gracefully, arcing proud and high into the morning sky, heading straight for 'Position A', miles down the middle of the fairway. His would be the best and longest drive seen all day from that tee. He would play a fabulous second shot into the green, and roll in his putt for a winning 'birdie' as if nothing in this world were more inevitable.

The almost 'otherworldly' character and strength he showed on the very first tee never faded throughout three astonishing days of competition. It inspired his fellow Europeans to the greatest heights, and positively awed the Americans. They truly never stood a chance.

Later that evening, on the peaceful veranda away from the team room, I asked Darren how he had coped with that first shot. 'I only had two choices,' he said, quietly. 'Either I did exactly what I wanted to do. Or I didn't.'

Darren's options were as stark and simple as that. They are for you, for me, for everyone.

Darren's Experience

In this true story, Darren was forced by sad circumstances into a miserable place. Clearly he had, at some point, to get himself out of there and improve his life. Having identified this, his choice was one of time: when would be the right time to start living a normal life. Would it be sooner or later?

Once he had taken the bull by the horns and chosen the 'sooner' option, he had to make himself commit to it. He still had a choice, as he himself said. He could give it 100 per cent full commitment and focus or he could go at it half-heartedly. Realistically, that left him with only one option! Only through total commitment would his mind and body automatically prepare for success: chemicals, muscles, instincts all working together to deliver the desired results.

And that's precisely what he did – although not without misgivings, of course. When something as traumatic as Darren experienced derails normal life, there is always the temptation to keep curled up in a protective 'ball'. We've all had those feelings of wanting to hide away and be 'small'. We feel exceptionally vulnerable because we've just taken a big hit. But when you do decide to crack on, you'll be wonderfully surprised by the support you get, sometimes from unexpected quarters.

You may have had to face trauma yourself. Often commitment and conviction to an end result allows you to have a purpose and that purpose may be enough to free you, even if just a little, from the anguish of your loss. That purpose may be in the form of justice, creating a legacy or achieving something now circumstances have changed. But, ultimately, it must be personal and emotionally important to you.

How to Commit to a Decision

Here's a big call. I think that decision making is not about understanding the choices and being able to predict success. Instead it is about being able to trust ourselves to navigate our way to a successful outcome.

We never have one choice to make in regard to a situation: it is never either 'this' or 'that'. For example, you may choose to leave a relationship, stay in the relationship and try to make it work, or move on from it. However, whatever the initial choice, you will only ever determine whether it was the right choice at a later stage, after making further decisions that stem from the original one.

Think about some successes in your life. Were they a result of your original decision? If you work backwards through each step that got you there, you'll find there were undoubtedly all sorts of twists and turns and possible outcomes along the way.

Because all 'big' decisions are dependent on so many seemingly smaller ones, there are many routes for us in life. In fact, there are so many permutations with regard to choice that it surely tells us it is not a matter of choosing 'the right path', but having the mindset that any path will be made to work for us, with options to change our path at many given opportunities.

Quickly think of a problem. For example, 'Shall I go to university or go out and get that job?' Next, quickly think of a solution. Now commit to that decision in your mind. Run through the course of events that your decision entails. If it seems like you've made the wrong decision, make different choices that allow it to work. Don't change the original decision. In your mind, commit to your decision and explore the various options that will make it the right one. Practise this, and prove to yourself that you get the outcome you want simply by committing to making decisions that take you to where you want to be.

The beauty of this technique is that it changes a mindset. Becoming decisive takes practise. You have to trust that you can make decisions without having all the facts. The only way to get that trust is to prove to yourself that whatever the consequences of your decisions, you have the capability to make further decisions that improve your situation.

You may wish to try this. Thinks of a decision you are trying to make.

'Shall I stay in this relationship or not?'
'Shall I set up my own business now?'
'Is now the time to go travelling?'
'Shall I try to build bridges with my parents?'

Toss a coin as if you really are going to commit to whichever one is chosen for you. As soon as you know, notice immediately how you feel. Are you elated? Saddened? Energised? Disappointed?

Imagine what the next step would be ... then the step after that. How do you feel? The same? Now imagine that it worked out and that at some stage in the future it really was the right decision to make. How would you feel and what did you have to do along the way to make it work?

You will probably find that there are a few routes to your success that spring to mind. This should only go to show that there is no clear path to your successful outcomes or even a clear strategy, just a willingness and determination to do what it takes to reach the result that is useful and beneficial to you.

Being able to commit to a decision comes from trust. Not trust that the decision is right, but trust that the decision can be made right. We cannot foretell the future, but we can shape it. This will come from living life with the correct attitude much more than using the best decision making process.

Points to Remember

- **Commitment can be a very liberating thing, be that in business, relationships or sport.** Gone are the doubts that stop you from putting all your energy behind any one decision, allowing all your efforts to be concentrated on making that choice the right one.

- **Commit fully to some small decisions, and realise you're doing it.** Let's say you want to take an hour out to watch television instead of doing a task that needs to be done. Well, if you do take that hour out, enjoy it! Don't sit there watching television and intermittently feeling bad. Enjoy it as your rest time and crack on with the task with the same commitment afterwards. You will notice a difference in how you feel.

- **There are no obstacles, only distractions.** No circumstance should interfere with your level of commitment. If you find yourself saying 'I'll try until I run out of money' or 'I'll try until my wife tells me to stop', or the very final excuse 'I'm too old now', then it's not commitment. 'I'll try until I succeed' is where your thoughts should be.

Once you choose your path, know the difference between something that blocks that particular route and something that just distracts you down another. Think now to something you've tried doing. Was the bad weather, economic conditions or the actions of others an obstacle, or merely the bright lights and ringing bells of a slot machine in the corner of the bar, catching your attention and taking your eye off the course of action you originally chose?

CHAPTER 4

Working the Confidence Muscle

Before you gain confidence you have to understand a little about what confidence is and what it looks like. This chapter will give you an insight into how confidence is something we can certainly control. Confidence is like many of the assets and attributes we already have. It is more than enough for us to dramatically achieve more, and in abundance.

What is Confidence?

Confidence is something we are all born with. To be confident is our natural state. To be confident is not the absence of fear; it is our feelings of self-belief and courage being stronger than any fear or apprehension we feel. Therefore fear, apprehension and anxiety cause us to be under-confident in a given situation when we feel those feelings to a greater extent than our confidence. If you imagine a time when you felt your confidence had gone or was lacking, it wasn't. Your confidence was the same as it always was, it's just that your fear was shouting louder.

Just look at young children and this is instantly obvious. They appear supremely confident, even over-confident. We only say 'over-confident' because we, as adults, have learnt that dangers lurk in life, and that we have to temper confidence with awareness.

When young children have no experience of fear associated with an action, they won't think twice about performing it. They don't, for instance, fear falling down when they are learning to walk. They don't have that far to fall anyway, and usually don't hurt themselves. And they certainly aren't afraid of making a fool of themselves! These are fears that we somehow acquire as we get older and more pompous. When we are old enough to allow something to dent our confidence, the depth of that dent is really determined by the significance we give to the event. Take, for example, something that once happened to me.

Back when I was just 14, I was asked to play the last post on a bugle at the local church in the Remembrance Sunday service. Maybe 'asked' isn't quite strong enough: people knew I was learning the trumpet and played a bugle in the Corps Band at school, so I was expected to comply, especially when the request came through my parents – laugh a minute, my childhood. They persuaded me that I'd enjoy it, so, to keep the peace, I agreed to perform, with the proviso that someone else played with me. But 'someone else' had stomach ache on the day in question, leaving Yours Truly up the creek without a mute.

When the moment came, I started off fine, and the bugle sounded fantastic in the church acoustics. But, about two-thirds of the way through, my mouth dried up, and all that came from my instrument was a pathetic, strangled farting noise. I tried again. More farts. Sweating profusely, I made a sign to the vicar as if to cut my throat, and slid shame-faced out of the building.

What significance did I attach to this balls-up? Considerable, is the answer. I could have simply thought, 'I bet hardly anyone noticed. Anyway what did they expect? Humphrey Lyttelton?' But no. A sense of perfectionism had been instilled into me by my parents. I felt ashamed – afraid to hold my head up. Even though my Dad assured me that he hardly noticed anything amiss at all – and that nobody else would have made much of it – I feared that everyone in the village would be staring at me and saying, 'Look! There's that lad who cocked up the last post in church the other day – what a failure!' So for a few weeks I stayed in a lot and kept my profile low. Missed out on fun. Felt a failure. And vowed never to perform in public on my own again (which I didn't).

Indeed, until I was at least 25 I never even spoke in front of an audience because I feared ridicule. I had allowed my confidence to be knocked quite badly by something relatively trivial and unimportant. Worse, most of this was in my head and not backed up by reality. I really believed my own interpretation of people's reactions, despite the fact that the truth – which completely vindicated my father's opinion – was plain to see!

This hypercritical perception of my own capabilities only changed when I became mature enough to appreciate that other people honestly felt I was good at getting a message across in public. They were not just saying it. I was still nervous, but their belief in me gradually overcame my own doubts. The crucial, additional spur was the audience reaction. I found I could make people listen and laugh *with* me, rather than (as I used to assume) at me! So, eventually, I began to positively look forward to performing.

All top performers – in business, sport and life – seem to have an inbuilt 'pressure regulator'. They can fine-tune it up or down in order to put themselves into the ideal performance state in which to achieve. They know that there is such a state applicable to everything they do – a window through which they can see success. They have the ability to both find it and then to open it.

What's Knocking Your Confidence?

It really helps to be able to identify – if you can remember that far back – what event or series of events knocked your confidence in an aspect of your life in the first place. Our fears are rarely completely irrational. Something – at some time – has stirred them. As time goes on, these fears – if they aren't addressed – gradually strengthen their grip and begin to show in undermining confidence.

How to Become More Confident

Most people are more confident in some areas of their lives than in others. Unless you have suffered a major emotional breakdown, which can knock confidence across the board, confidence is usually selective. In a bizarre way, this is a good thing. It means that we can look at ourselves and see that we have areas of strong confidence as well as weak ones. We can recognise that we're not entirely useless, and that there are things we can do to alter our confidence levels if we wish.

Some people are happy to accept that they have areas of low confidence and not worry about it. That sort of acceptance actually signifies that – overall – a person is pretty confident! However, if a lack of confidence is seriously affecting our ability to live a normal life – or affecting our nearest and dearest – then maybe we should aim to improve matters.

Remember, whatever you do, it doesn't need to happen all at once. You can increase your confidence gradually just by pushing your boundaries a tiny bit further each time you try something. Just as with physical exercise, you are better off starting slowly and building up your efforts gradually to avoid doing yourself harm. It might sound corny, but it's true – you can think of your confidence as a muscle. The more you exercise that confidence muscle, the stronger it becomes.

You *must* remember that you are not alone. It is an exceedingly rare person who retains his or her confidence in all aspects of life. Everybody has a weakness, and often people's weaknesses lie in things that others around them assume are strengths! That's because we all cover up our weaknesses, often very well. Furthermore, we tend to assume that because someone seems very confident in one respect that this confidence must inevitably spill over into the rest of what they do. Not true!

We all know people who are brash, a bit loud and 'braggy'. They can seem rude and arrogant to those who can't see through their 'act'. They like to show us this apparent confidence when, in reality, they are hiding behind a shell. When you are truly confident, you don't feel any need to shout about it. You simply let your actions speak for themselves.

Just like an alcoholic, you can only begin rebuilding lost confidence when you can admit truthfully to yourself that you need help in some aspect of your life. So go on – like a car with spots of rust that need repairing, start identifying your weak areas. Then work on them, bit by bit. Exercise your confidence muscle gradually, and soon you'll turn your weaknesses into strengths. Trust me, it works.

Visualise the Perfect You

It is important to try and make our feelings tangible. We all want to feel confident, but what does confidence really look like?

Visualise what you would look like if you were super-confident. Close your eyes and give yourself a minute to picture the perfect you walking into your local pub, or going from the car park into the office. If you were the perfect you, how would you be walking? What would you be wearing? What is your hair doing? How fast or slow are you going? Where are you looking? Most importantly, what are you feeling? Notice all the changes in your demeanour and body language as you build a picture of the confident you.

Once we've seen this enough times, and really understood the picture, we can replicate it so much more easily.

How to Be a Confident Performer

At some time or other, just about all of us experience that horrible, sinking feeling in the pit of the stomach when someone suggests that we stand up and speak in public. It's just not something that comes naturally to many of us, which means that we have to learn how to do it. Honestly, it's not that hard when we break it all down.

I guess what we all dread is that we'll simply 'dry up' – be left, standing there, with all eyes upon us, unable to remember what we wanted to say in the first place. Or that what we do say simply doesn't come out right and makes us sound stupid. Or that we *do* say it right, but that none of the audience agrees with it. Even worse, they might not even understand our point, and we end up being faced with a sea of blank, uncomprehending looks.

In some ways it's worse if you agree to speak in a way that is supposed to be entertaining, like a best man's speech. Traditionally, everyone expects your speech to be a series of hilarious recollections, dubious stories, witty ripostes to drunken, heckling wedding guests and corny jokes. But what if they don't find anything funny? Do you laugh at your own lines? Do you mumble something about 'Well, it seemed funny at the time' and stumble sheepishly on? Or what if you let slip some risqué story about the groom's past that immediately generates steely expressions and a 20-degree drop in temperature from the parents and in-laws, and you end up feeling about as welcome as a fart in a space suit?

Then there's acting (well, it's all about acting, as I'll explain in a bit – but I mean being in a play or a panto or something). You worry about forgetting your lines, missing all your cues, being in the wrong place on the stage at the wrong time.

There are several vital things you really must try and remember in virtually all of these cases. The first is that **very few people in the audience would actually choose to swap places with you** when you are up there, exposed and vulnerable. The vast majority of people will feel exactly as you do about getting up on their hind legs and spouting! Not many of us relish the prospect because we don't want to make ourselves look silly in public. But as long as we accept the idea that everyone else knows how hard it is to be in the spotlight, we must also try and appreciate that there will be a lot of natural empathy in the audience. **Just as long as you make a genuine effort, and try your best, decent people will be sympathetic to the odd stumble.** They will usually be willing you to put your case across well (even if they don't agree with it).

Sure, you'll get the occasional idiot who will shout out stupid comments – someone who is too much of a coward to ever get up there and do it themselves. But that's life. It contains a certain percentage of idiots – it says so on the pack. Don't be fazed by them. Ignore them or, if that doesn't work and you're brave enough, call their bluff. 'I'm sorry if I'm interrupting you ... would you like to come up here and speak first?' I assure you that you will be guaranteed to get the rest of the audience on your side in an instant!

As I tell many of my corporate clients, **remember that your audience is human too.** The majority will appreciate your guts in standing up there, and will understand your fears. If you do stumble or lose your way, be honest. Own up ... and smile, if you can. Be as natural as if you were in a small group in the pub: 'Damn! I've forgotten what I was going to say. Oh yes ... I remember.' Then just carry on. **Nobody is recording your performance and expecting one, flawless 'take'.** They'll simply pick up with you where you left off. Don't race away at 100mph – take your time, remember to breathe, speak as loudly and clearly as you can, and don't gabble or mumble into your beard (especially not if you're a woman).

Preparation is Everything

Okay, that's the actual performance bit sorted, but what comes before that is every bit as important. It's what makes you – as a public speaker or performer – exactly like an Olympic athlete, Formula One racing driver or international footballer. You'll stand far less chance of coming a cropper if you've done your homework properly. **Preparation is everything.** Of course, top sports and business people have heaps of drive, energy and natural talent, but think of the number of times you see hugely talented people doing nothing with these God-given attributes. The ones who manage to really shine and stand out are those who have put in the hard yards in terms of practise and preparation. No amount of natural ability will make you a consistent star if you do no background work at all.

So, in my experience, one massive reason why most people are so apprehensive about making speeches is that they simply don't allow themselves enough time to prepare their material. You have to be sure that you are going to be saying the right things in the right order – whether it's joking or serious – and that you have remembered everything. The next vital point is that you need to **be sure that what you want to say actually works when it is spoken out loud.** So many times we write stuff down on the PC, or on a scrap of paper, that makes sense when we read it to ourselves. But when we actually try and read it out loud, it loses all of its impact, or it is really hard to follow. So physically rehearse your speech … to the cat, to a teddy bear, to the television screen or to a long-suffering friend or relative.

Confidence is all about feeling comfortable in your surroundings. Once you have reached a point at which you are happy with your material, you will feel far more confident about standing up before an audience and spouting. And once you are able to accept that they are – fundamentally – on your side (even if they disagree with details of content), you will feel far more comfortable and less concerned about making a fool of yourself.

Talking Confidently on the Phone

We all have to speak on the phone a lot these days. Confidence comes into it in a big way, even if you don't realise it, especially when you are speaking to someone you don't know. This can be particularly important both in a work context (notably in a sales environment), and when trying to get a relationship going (plucking up the courage to ask someone out).

For some reason, we seem to assume that people won't want to speak to us or listen to what we have to say. Consequently, we worry about many of the same things that we do when public speaking. We get tongue-tied and, because we can't actually see the face of the person we're calling, our attention can easily wander. It is much harder to communicate without visual cues, and much easier for us to be misunderstood. It's obvious, really – we simply can't see if someone is smiling, surprised or curious a lot of the time.

So how can we boost our confidence on the phone? I always tell people to **try and remember to *sound* confident**, because even if you're actually a bag of nerves, the person on the other end of the line can't see that. The one thing few of us use to full effect is light and shade in our voices. Because we can't see facial expressions, we should try and replace them with vocal expressions to give better clues as to what we really mean by our words. When I first did some radio broadcasting, I was told to literally grin like an idiot as I was talking! Clearly, you don't do this if the subject matter is very grave, but if you are engaged in a friendly chat, **physically grinning gives your voice a real 'sparkle'**. Try it – you'll be amazed at how well this works!

Your appearance counts for nothing when you are using the phone. So if you are under-confident about how you look, but you have a great voice, people will respond amazingly well. Some people have fantastic voices: I have known several cases where two people have fallen in love purely through talking to each other, even though they would probably not have given each other a second look! So **your voice is an immensely powerful tool** – neglect it at your peril.

Many people hate hearing the sound of their own voice – they become petrified as soon as there's a microphone within 100 yards! We're not talking about being on the radio or anything like that – simply putting a message on the home answer phone is enough to throw most of us. The thing is, we hardly ever get the chance to hear ourselves as others hear us and, whenever we do, we hate what we hear. 'I don't really sound like that, do I?' People can't believe that their accent is that noticeable, that strong, and neither can they believe that they sound so *dull* and expressionless most of the time!

'Tweak' Your Voice

To help you use your voice to its full potential, I suggest you do a little homework. Practise listening to yourself and literally 'tweaking' your voice until it sounds how you want it to sound. Use an old tape recorder if necessary, and just have some fun practising a little. It only needs a few minutes a day.

The more we can be sure of saying what we want to say, saying it how we want to say it, and sounding how we want to sound, the more confident we will be when interacting with other people. This involves good preparation, and taking real note of the physical quality of our message. Confidence is, in many ways, a bit of a con itself. The truth is, **if you sound confident – whether you can be seen or not – other people assume that you *are* confident.** The whole process generates a positive feedback loop which, in turn, genuinely bolsters and enhances your actual confidence.

I often tell golfers I deal with to **'walk the walk' and look the part**, even if they don't feel like it at the time. For professional sports and business people and amateurs alike, looking the business is halfway towards doing it!

DAN'S STORY

While we were playing cricket together, a friend told me a story about an American television presenter. Jim, my friend, had worked in New York for a couple of years. During this period, he and his journalist fiancée Linda were invited to a 30-somethings' Christmas lunch party at Mac and Bev's – a couple he had got to know well. After a huge lunch, the guests were sprawling in the lounge with wine and chocolate, while a widescreen plasma television burbled to itself in the corner. A 'celebrity' presenter was hosting some feel-good show helping underprivileged kids live their dreams.

Jim hated these plastic celebrities – he always had. I suspected deep-rooted jealousy was behind his sarcasm. 'All he does is grin like a chimp and prattle on about nothing – bet he gets paid a bloody fortune too!'

It transpired that Mac thought the same. Bev had only made things worse by commenting on his handsome appearance – 'Good-looking guy, isn't he?' – provoking Mac into a vitriolic attack on the poor bloke. Having accused him of looking like some 'Joe 90' with an orange, sun-bed complexion, he had finished him off with what Jim described as his usual, not-so-subtle *coup de grâce*: 'Dan bloody Shepherd: bet he's gay, anyway.' I honestly don't remember the man's real name, but 'Dan' will do as well as any.

Rolling her eyes upwards to the ceiling as if she'd heard it all before (which she had), Bev had steamed in on Dan's behalf. Or 'Danny boy', as she'd called him, much to Mac's derision, who had then accused her of fancying him. With the wine bottle circulating, Bev had leaned forward conspiratorially to embark upon a fascinating insight into Dan, the man on the box.

Apparently, Bev had used to live next door to him when they were all kids down in Richmond – him and his big brother Neil. She insisted that she had never fancied him as he was far too young then, but admitted that she was in awe of his ability to get into – and out of – spectacular scrapes!

'There was a time when he lost his temper with Neil and was chasing him round and round the house,' Bev explained. He was careering through the front door, out the back, up the driveway in a mad loop, yelling all sorts of unprintable curses. Eventually, he'd started catching up because Neil couldn't stop laughing. They'd both come flying round the front – Neil had got back in the door and slammed it shut just before Dan had arrived. They had glass front doors in their street and Dan couldn't stop. So he went through the door – literally. There was a huge crash – glass everywhere – and a big hole shaped like Dan! 'Everyone just held their breath.'

Bev explained that Dan simply appeared to have no fear. He had walked away from the glass door incident with just one tiny scratch, and had then proceeded to get himself entangled in another potential disaster only two weeks later. Surely, I was thinking, there couldn't be more. I mean, most of us learn our lesson after one or, at the most, two reckless episodes, don't we? I'd said as much to Jim, who insisted that worse was to come and carried on. Dan, it seems, had decided to see what the view was like from the top of his house. He'd seen some programme on television about climbing Everest, apparently. The first Bev had known about all this was when she'd heard a cry of 'Bev! Bev!' When she had looked round into their drive, there was Dan, halfway up a drainpipe made out of plastic sections. She had yelled to him to get down, 'cos it looked really dangerous', but he wouldn't have it. He'd just kept on shinning up until, when he was nearly at the top by the gutter, one of the sections had broken away from the house wall. Then the whole lot had come crashing down 'like in slow motion'. Dan, said Bev, was still clinging on to the top section of pipe when he'd hit the concrete drive nearly 30 feet below.

By now, apparently, Mac had pulled on some ludicrous red trunks over his jeans and was standing in an astonishingly silly 'superhero' pose with matching accent: 'I guess I just kinda walked away, like any other self-respecting, indestructible superhero would.' Jim said that he had got a vague idea that Bev might almost 'hold a candle' for Dan Shepherd. No wonder Mac was irritated – it must have seemed like a meeting of his official fan club. Then Bev had got annoyed at the way the two lads were 'taking the mickey', and had challenged them to be as confident as Dan. 'He just oozes it, doesn't he? Think of it – in front of all those cameras and how many million viewers? Could you do it?'

'Piece of cake' had been Mac's flip reply. A fine one, too, until Bev had pointed out to everyone that prior to a recent presentation at work, Mac hadn't slept for a week. He then couldn't eat for two days, and was sick three times before he got into the meeting. And that was presenting to only *five* people! No, it certainly appeared that Dan had a rare gift of confidence, and both Mac and Jim were green with envy. Until, Jim said, his fiancée had thrown them all a 'curve ball'.

Linda – a magazine journalist – would do that, apparently: take everything in, not say a word for ages then hit nails on heads with devastating accuracy. She had coolly explained that both boys feared rejection which, as 'macho' men, they had naturally denied vehemently. She had also mentioned that – before she had met Jim – she had actually interviewed Dan Shepherd, and that she could say, categorically, that he wasn't gay! Mac, being Mac, had assumed that this meant something had gone on between the two of them – a notion Linda had very quickly squashed.

She had, it seemed, asked Dan some highly personal questions which he had answered very honestly. No, he wasn't gay, but he was extremely under-confident when it came to relationships with women. In fact – Linda had continued – he would have loved to have married someone he had met years ago. There was a girl he had once adored – absolutely adored – yet he had never dared reveal his true feelings to her in case she had laughed at him. So she never knew how Dan had felt. 'She probably still doesn't.' He had said it really was years ago. He was infatuated, and had never felt quite the same about anyone else after that. 'Apparently, she used to live next door.'

I remember thinking what a spooky ending that was when Jim told me the story. It still gets me now, not least because of the fact that even an apparently super-confident soul like Dan could still have one weakness that could betray a big part of his life. So there's still hope for us all. We all have room for improvement, and that's got to be a positive view.

Dan's Experience

In reminiscing about what Dan was like as a lad, Bev is highlighting the fact that he knew no fear. He got into some horrendous scrapes, but, because he didn't attach massive significance to what happened, he didn't allow them to dent his confidence. Goodness only knows why, but some people are like that!

The accidents he had would have added to his database of 'potentially dangerous situations' somewhere in the depths of his brain. This would mean, for example, that next time he was considering climbing something high and relatively flimsy, he would be aware of the potential consequences of falling off. He would know that pain would probably result, and might moderate his behaviour as a result. But he would-n't allow himself to get too paranoid – too fearful – of heights in general. That's because of the lack of real signifi-cance he attached to the event. Other people in his position might have attributed a much greater importance to what had happened, which might – in turn – translate into a morbid fear of heights full stop: ladders, escalators, lifts, high buildings, even flying.

So Dan's innate confidence – tempered by cautionary expe-rience – remained intact. Clearly, too, this confidence carried over into performing in public. Unlike many people, he was comfortable and relaxed in front of a camera, microphone, studio audience and – potentially – several million viewers. Anybody would be forgiven for assuming that this was a super-confident man without a care in the world. However ...

When Linda had interviewed him years earlier – just as he was becoming known for his media work, but wasn't yet a 'celebrity' – she had established a good rapport. Good enough to elicit some surprising answers to cheeky personal questions! What these answers showed was that far from being super-confident in all walks of life, Dan – like most of us – had areas of weak personal confidence. If we were Mac or Jim (not to mention Bev), we would probably be gob-smacked that someone who could act as Dan did on primetime television shows could possibly doubt himself when it came to the fairer sex. Yet he did – to such an extent that his lack of confidence had quite probably been the cause of a huge void in his life.

We might think Dan had everything, but he knew he lacked the one thing he craved most of all. It just goes to show that we are all pretty good at covering up, and fairly bad at seeing through the 'fronts' that others put on. We should never base our behaviour purely on assumptions about other people because we are far too easily surprised. Just remember that confidence rarely encompasses every single part of anyone's life. Remember, too, that it was always there to begin with. It may take a little time and effort, but confidence can always be restored.

Fill Yourself with Confidence

This visualisation exercise is designed to help you gain confidence in all aspects of your life.

Start by ensuring you are in a quiet room with no potential distractions, such as television, phones or music. Close your eyes. Take your time and, with every successive breath, try to relax a little deeper. Enjoy how amazingly relaxed you can become as you allow each muscle to switch off and melt away, one by one.

Once you have settled into that lovely, loose, limp, lazy feeling – and your breathing has that wonderful sleepy 'ebb and flow' rhythm – imagine a huge glass jug above your head.

Now start to fill the jug with every compliment ever said to you, every single word of praise. Imagine it start to fill and, as it does, think of it turning a colour of your choosing. This can be any colour you like, but one you can associate with confidence.

Simply remember anything that ever made you feel great that your parents, friends, teachers or even strangers said to you, or about you. Really think back. It might even be something nice you said yourself when you passed that exam, stood up to that bully or spoke your mind to your parents! Just make sure that the jug is filling to the brim with everything that ever made you feel great.

Now, once you're smiling and almost ready to burst with how wonderful you feel when you recall all that great stuff, pile in some more! Think of it as a super-concentrated, delicious 'smoothie'. With each compliment, smile, remember and enjoy the 'well dones', and allow yourself to feel it all over again – only this time, like the smoothie, super-concentrated.

Once the jug is brimming with all that feel-good colour of confidence, count slowly in your mind. Three, two, one …

Then pour it all over you and let it splash down triumphantly, like some winning racing driver has shaken up a magnum of champagne and deluged you in the froth, bubbles and fantastic taste of success.

Imagine being soaked through – drenched – as it splashes on to your head, down your face and on to your chest, and imagine just how incredible it feels to get every single compliment ever paid to you all at the same time! Let it soak you right through to the bone, as if each muscle and organ is simply infused with liquid confidence. Allow it to course through your veins and arteries, and enjoy the intensely powerful feelings of self-belief and happiness that you can create deep within yourself.

As you enjoy these delightful feelings rushing around inside you, think of yourself saturated from the inside out in the colour you imagined. Then open your eyes.

The trick is to allow yourself to feel this good when you're tackling a daunting chore or task you've got coming up. Imagine this fantastic feeling of knowing that you're impressing both other people and yourself. You know that you're performing as well as you possibly can – as well as anyone could in your situation. You feel completely comfortable in your own skin at those moments when it matters most. Feel that relaxed, peaceful, inward smile that comes with the knowledge that you're making the very most out of every drop of confidence you have ever experienced. Now think about the task.

Doing a Presentation

Imagine the presentation you soon have to do at work, the one that you're secretly quite anxious about. Think of standing in front of that important group of people, and imagine how your confidence can change their perceptions. Drench yourself in your colour – let's say it's purple. Watch as these people pour themselves glasses of water and – in your mind – it all comes out in a deep, rich shade of blackcurrant. Watch them sip it and drink in your confidence. Don't worry – the supply is endless, and there's plenty for everyone! Now every single person in your focus is on your side, and you can win the day.

Making a Long Journey

Imagine the long motorway drive you have to make next week. Normally you hate the claustrophobia of being in a seemingly interminable traffic jam, and get tense and anxious just thinking about that possibility. Not now, though. Just before you join the motorway, you press the screen-wash button and guess what? Your cleaning fluid is a wonderful purple (but not too opaque so you can't see clearly), and it cleans astonishingly fast and efficiently. You feel invigorated and fresh, especially when you notice all the other drivers around you cleaning their screens with your fabulous purple confidence! So not only are you feeling good, you can sense that they are, too. All of a sudden, everyone knows that you are performing at your peak, and they're thrilled for you.

Going to a Party

Then there's that party that you've been committed to attending by your 'other half'. Perhaps you're a bit on the shy side and not really a party person, and the last thing you want is to walk into a room full of strangers and have to make polite conversation. But you ring the doorbell, you are welcomed warmly and shown in, and the hostess is wearing a fabulous purple dress. In fact, there's purple everywhere: the gin and tonic in your hand becomes spectacularly transformed. You feel completely at home, relaxed and comfortable – conversation comes easily, as do smiles and good wishes from everyone you meet.

All you ever have to do is to remember that fantastic feeling of being drenched from head to foot by this astonishing jug of unlimited, feel-good, purple confidence that should almost be part of your DNA. If there is ever anything you are anxious about doing, or people you are nervous about meeting, think of that amazing liquid coursing through your veins. Imagine it all around you, protecting you and stimulating you to excel. Trust in yourself, and in all those positive judgements people have made about you in the past. Believe in yourself, and in your power to live up to realistic expectations. Think your confidence colour, and put the world on your side!

Points to Remember

- **You have not lost confidence. It's just hiding under a few things.** No matter how many times clients have sat in front of me and said they have no confidence, I am always able to find them exhibiting confidence in some area of their life. So let's accept you are not unconfident, but that you are capable of being unconfident. Someone much wiser than I once said that 'people are not evil; they are capable of being evil'. Now this allows us to separate the act from the person, and you must do this with the times you are not confident.

- **The more you acquire strength from realising and acknowledging when you are the person you wish to be, the more your confidence will grow.** It is possible to transfer that good feeling into other areas of your life. Confidence can be used wherever you like – if you know how to do it in one place, you can do it in another.

CHAPTER 5

Embrace Your Fear

THINK OF A fear ... The thing is, you're not. You're thinking of spiders, flying, lack of money, being alone ... These
things are animals, incidents, situations, etc. They also don't
hold fear for some people. In this chapter let's not just
understand the principle of fear, but go one better. I aim to
show you how fear is nothing to be scared of. In fact, if we
understand more about this powerful emotion, we can
harness the useful information we get from it.

If you think of the human body as a computer, a part of
our most primitive 'operating system' has the fear response
built into it. Instinctively, our bodies know what to do when
faced with something threatening. Fear sets off a stream of
chemical reactions which enable us to 'fight or flee': adrena-
lin is released, the heart rate quickens and muscles are
readied for explosive action should it prove necessary.
Effectively, we put ourselves on red alert.

So, at the most basic level, we are programmed to respond to threat. But what we don't know – until we learn it – is how to label any given event or situation as 'threatening'. A newborn baby, for example, will not be afraid of fire. Going back to the computer analogy, we are also born with a brain that acts as a sort of 'virus scanner'. This helps us begin to learn to label what we experience on a day-to-day basis as 'threatening' or 'non-threatening' and add it to our database of knowledge.

Actually, some of this database is already in the scanner, learnt by our entire human species over millions of years and genetically passed down the line. There is also a sort of 'herd instinct' learning that happens almost automatically. A baby will quickly discover from people around it that fire is a potential danger: everyone else seems to be wary of that orange flame, so it should be, too. Either that, or it will learn from direct personal experience: 'I see. If I put my hand in that orange flame, it feels hot and, shortly afterwards, it hurts. A lot!' Similarly, a baby will learn to identify aggression and the threat it might pose.

Fear is a natural, basic response that is good for us. According to what our database tells us, it mobilises instinctive mind and body reactions, and saves our lives every day. The last thing we would want to do is eliminate our capacity to fear. **The trouble with fear is not fear itself, but the way we apply the labels. Quite simply, we get things wrong sometimes.** We spend a great deal of time worrying about things, half of which will never happen.

Get a piece of paper and write down at least 10 things you once feared. Did your fears turn out to be unfounded for most of these things? It's likely that they weren't anywhere near as scary as you thought.

Everyone is different, yet – through the 'herd instinct' type of learning – we take on board lots of threat labels that often don't apply to us. For example, most people shudder when you talk about a visit to the dentist, or having to get up and speak in public. If you'd never been exposed to these common anxieties before, you'd make your own mind up based on your personal experience. But you don't. If you have to do something that people, generally, see as vaguely threatening, you go into it with your mind already half made up. You're thinking, 'I should be apprehensive of this. Something bad could happen. Everybody says so.' You are on edge to start with when, really, you shouldn't be. So when you are sitting in the dentist's chair, you are so tuned up to expect pain that you almost imagine it, or jump out of your seat at the slightest twinge! This, of course, doesn't make the dentist's job any easier, and it's more likely that you will cause something painful to happen.

Understanding Our Fears

What we must try to do is understand more clearly why we are experiencing fear. Is it really appropriate to you as an individual in a given situation? And, if it is, listen logically to what it is telling you, rather than instinctively panicking! Think of your fears as friendly voices in your head – helpful voices seeking to guide you, rather than instructions being barked out at you on a parade ground.

You see, it's incredibly hard to try and change the way we feel. This means that if we feel anxious about something, it's really difficult to ignore that feeling. What's so much easier for us to do is to accept – embrace – the fear, and remember that our fears are totally – 100 per cent – on our side. We are always on our own side. For example, if you were ill, your body would be fighting that illness no matter what. So, think of the fear you 'hear' in your head as saying precisely the right thing, even if it is doing so at an awkward time in the wrong way, a bit like having a loyal five-year-old child at your side. If you have children, you can relate to the fact that although they are on your side, they may not articulate things well from time to time. Let's say you're in the egg and spoon race with your five-year-old son or daughter. They may be shouting at you: 'Don't drop it! Don't trip over!' Now, when you're trying to complete a task the last thing you need is that negative imagery, but at the end of the day, all they want you to do is succeed so you forgive them.

Picture yourself in the egg and spoon race. Think about how you would handle a five-year-old coming out with these things. You'd probably say something like, 'Thank you, I'll concentrate!'

Turning Your Fears to Your Advantage

The important thing is to listen to the fear in your head, rationalise it and take its advice. What we usually do, however, is allow this voice to terrorise us. We get all hot and clammy and worry about that voice in our head being right: 'You're not good enough', 'Who do you think you are?', 'You'll make fool of yourself in that meeting', and so on. But it is possible to rationalise these fears and benefit from them. Say you hear a voice saying, 'Don't forget your lines ... don't forget your lines.' The response you need to give is, 'Thank you, you're right, I'm glad I prepared properly.' Similarly, 'Don't blush when you walk into this meeting' becomes 'Thank you, you're right, I'll walk into this meeting confidently.' 'Don't kick the ball over the crossbar' becomes 'Thank you, you're right, I'll pick my target, concentrate on it and focus on completing the task.'

The subconscious mind does not hear the word 'don't' or 'not'. If, for example, you are trying to give up smoking, the worst thing you could be saying to yourself is, 'I am not a smoker.' We are simply drawn towards our most dominant thoughts. All your subconscious mind will be hearing is the word 'smoker'. It's a bit like the old 'don't think of a pink elephant' thing. The brain has to construct a thought in order to deconstruct it. We must think of what we are not supposed to think about! Stick with me on this ...

USING THE LANGUAGE OF SUCCESS

Which words are mainly in your head? Are they words based around fear ('redundancy', 'bankruptcy', 'alone', 'embarrassment') or success ('promotion', 'bonus' and so on)? If you want to speak the language of success rather than the language of fear, 'I am not a smoker' becomes 'I enjoy having healthy lungs and breathing fresh air.'

Let's say that you start up a business. What sort of language will determine your motivation? Will it be the language of fear?

> 'This business has got to work because if it doesn't I could go bankrupt.'

> 'This business has got to work because if it doesn't my friends will laugh at me.'

> 'This business has got to work because if it doesn't I'll have to downsize the car.'

> 'This business has got to work because if it doesn't we may lose the house.'

Alternatively, will it be the language of success and achievement?

> 'When this business works out I'm going to upgrade the house.'

> 'When this business works out, I'm going to buy a holiday home in Florida.'

'When this business works out, I'm going to take three days off a week to spend with the kids.'

'When this business works out, I'm going on a cruise.'

Imagine how you would feel if the dominant words and pictures in your head were in the language of aspiration and achievement. Then think about how this would change if these words and pictures were in the language of fear.

Allow negative thoughts into your mind rather than trying to banish them. Once they're there, simply work with them to help yourself. Try and interact rationally with the voice, rather than getting angry, frustrated or panicky. In this way, your fears stop being your focus and drop into the background of your thoughts. Once there, they carry on quietly helping you do what you really want to do.

CHRIS'S STORY

The lady sitting next to me on a recent flight to New York had caught my eye after we'd been airborne about 20 minutes. A coy smile, then she'd looked away. Soon afterwards I had managed to drop a load of magazines and papers at her feet as I was trying to arrange myself for the journey. As I started to gather them up again, she moved in her seat to allow me some more space, then bent forward to help. She picked up the substantial sheaf of paper-clipped documents that was furthest from my reach, and couldn't resist a cursory glance at the title page. It was a draft script for a television show I was about to rehearse.

She smiled and made a light-hearted comment about sharing with a celebrity, then asked if I was *the* Jamil Qureshi. 'The very same,' I replied, joining in this gentle banter, although mystified as to how she knew my name. Realising this, she explained that it was on the script. 'Aah … so you'll be Agatha Christie, then,' but she wasn't. She had to ask me what I did, and I don't imagine Agatha would have needed to do that.

Having settled back into my seat, I had to think hard. Where to begin? I said that I tried to cope with my fear of flying. That I appeared on television as a sort of resident psychologist from time to time, helping people sort out life issues. That I helped professional sports people to think like winners, and business people to think like high achievers and great managers … Here, she interrupted me. 'You don't help singer–songwriters to overcome stage fright then?'

That sounded interesting. After all, stage fright is the same for everyone – you don't have to be famous or work in a glamorous job to get it. At some time or other, many of us will have to make a 'best man's' speech, or give a presentation of some sort at work. When you think about it, ringing up a stranger on the phone – if you're in sales, say, and new to it all – could just as easily generate something amounting to the same. I was sure I could help her, but admitted that I hadn't tackled her specific problem before. Well, I'd never met a proper singer–songwriter, and there was something about her that made me think she was probably quite well known. Maybe I was the one sitting next to the celebrity! She quickly denied this possibility, explaining that I wouldn't have heard any of her stuff as she'd not released anything for years. I wondered why this was, and she said that it was a long and boring story. As we faced a long and boring flight anyway, I invited her to tell me.

It seemed that she and her partner had separated a few years back. They used to perform together. He did most of the writing, and she just sang with him. After the split, she wrote a handful of songs on her own, and did one short tour. But then she 'sort of seemed to gradually freeze'. She began to dread performing her songs on her own. She'd get stage fright, too – really badly – which was when she decided to pack it all in. But I still didn't know who she was, so I asked. 'Oh, yes. Sorry – it's Christine. Chris.'

She continued, saying that she couldn't get her head round the fact that it hadn't always been like that. Years ago it never bothered her – she used to be able to sing like a bird at the drop of a hat. As a small girl she would just get up on the stage and sing her heart out: at school, at weddings, at kids' parties – even for singing exams.

But, I supposed, she would always have sung material written by other people? 'Always,' she replied, surprised that I might find this nugget relevant. I asked her about her stage fright in detail. Did she think she'd forget the songs? The words? The chords? Was it the thought of having to engage with an audience on her own? Could she put her finger on exactly what would bother her the most?

She supposed it was all of those things, but that now I had made her think about it, they seemed sort of secondary. Although she'd never really worked it out before, she reckoned that what she probably feared most was that people wouldn't actually like the songs. But hadn't they always liked them before? Yes, she said, but *before*, someone else had always taken responsibility for writing them. They were never hers, never a part of her soul. And she supposed that if people were thinking, 'Uh, that song's crap,' then they would be thinking she was crap, and she'd begin to feel she had no right being up on stage in the spotlight.

That's when the communication bit would go AWOL, and she'd mumble something garbled and rush into the next song which, I guessed, might then start off at half-cock, and the audience would pick up on her anxiety? She agreed enthusiastically.

I seemed to be on the right track here. I was beginning to suspect that all Chris might need was a nudge in the right direction ... and that I might just be about to add 'singer–songwriters' to my CV.

I agreed completely with a further observation of Chris's when she made the comparison between an audience and an animal: that they can both smell fear. I confessed to knowing that feeling only too well, explaining that for ages I used to feel exactly the same anxieties that she'd just described before I had to speak in public. Especially if I was supposed to make it funny! She wondered how I had got around the problem, whether I had a guru to help me. I said that some good people gave me really solid advice, and things began to make sense, bit by bit. They had told me I was pretty good at it – when I got going – so I figured that maybe my fears were a bit over the top. I added that being a perfectionist didn't help much, either, because if I made so much as the slightest cock-up compared to what I saw as the 'perfect performance', I used to imagine that it would stand out like a sore thumb.

'When I bet nobody noticed at all!' said Chris. Already she seemed a lot happier talking about all this. I told her that I gradually dropped my standards – which were plainly absurdly high – and found I could skate over a few minor blemishes without them throwing me. And that I was able to relax more, which helped amazingly in improving my rapport with the crowd. She immediately appeared to understand, saying that it all made a lot of sense.

Well, it's obvious – to you, to me, to anyone – when it's all laid out in front of us. All it takes is for someone to give us the clarity to see it. The message I passed on to Chris was that she shouldn't let her fears get all her focus. Sure, they'd always be there – in the background – which is no bad thing, because there's usually an element of truth in all our fears. In her case, I continued, all her fears were actually saying was, 'Chris, for God's sake, make sure you're completely happy with the songs you decide to perform.'

Chris was now grinning broadly. She caught the attention of a passing flight attendant, and called for some 'champagne for my guru'. I was delighted that she could now see her problem in such a different light. She vowed to prepare more carefully, and be more selective about the set lists she created. She said that, if she did that, there was no way stage fright should stop her any more. Something must have worked, because she has since made three delightful CDs, all released to rave reviews, and all her own work. Thanks to Chris I actually enjoyed the flight – and that's not something that happens very often.

Chris's Experience

Fear is an essential part of performance: because it is natural and within us, like our physiology and chemistry, it's on our side.

Great performers do not have an ability to control or subdue their feelings: they have an ability to channel them. By Chris understanding what she was feeling and why she was feeling it, she was able to reframe the experience and use it to her advantage.

Feelings are relative to the individual. Singers, soldiers or shop assistants all feel fear as much as each other, but what allows perfect performance is understanding how fear helps.

Face Your Fears

Don't ever think that 'super-performers' don't feel fear. Everyone does. The most successful people on the planet have phone calls they don't want to make, and meetings they don't want to go to. You may be familiar with Dr Susan Jeffers' book *Feel the Fear and Do it Anyway*. The title is one of the best ever for a self-help book.

Think about a time you did something that you feared. It makes no difference how big or small this thing is – if you feared it, it was big! This might just be parking your spouse's car, or walking into that room full of strangers when you so easily could have gone home. Turn your television off and watch the blank screen. Imagine that you are watching yourself on the television, handling this situation brilliantly. Be amazed as you watch yourself, an ordinary person, doing an extraordinary thing.

Enjoy how wonderful you are, and notice your demeanour and body language as you deal with your fear. As you watch yourself on the screen, understand what you were thinking, and how that translated to your behaviours and actions. (Well done you, by the way.)

Now, you can repeat this any time you wish: just turn off

the television and watch yourself confidently handling situations you fear. Let it become your own little practice area. Feel free to wind forward and back, zoom in and out, slow down or speed up, and change the camera angle. Just make sure you get a very clear look at you handling your fear situations brilliantly in advance. Know what you look like at your best and re-create it.

Points to Remember

- **Courage is not the absence of fear,** but the wisdom to act even though you feel it.
- **Start to enjoy the nervousness of performing certain tasks.** Get used to the feeling of nervousness and try to understand why you feel it. Once you've done that you're free to work out how it could help.
- **Choose someone you admire and be in their shoes.** How would Richard Branson handle feeling like this before the meeting? Try to act out the role of being the person you wish to become. Take note of your demeanour and body language.
- **Pat yourself on the back when you do the thing that you fear.** The more you acknowledge your ability to perform when feeling fear, the less hold fear has over you. Like dealing with a bully, it seems with fear that the more you allow yourself to be bullied, the more bullied you become. Do the thing that you fear and watch the fear diminish.

CHAPTER 6

That's Life ... Accept It!

THINGS HAPPEN IN life that we don't like. Fact. Much of the time, there's absolutely nothing we can do about them. They're out of our control but they affect what we do, how we behave and the decisions we make. These things often take us by surprise – we can't always predict them. Yet that's life: its very unpredictability is ... predictable!

There will be occasions when electricians don't turn up on time, and when we're cut up on the way to work. And it will rain – despite what the forecast said – when we don't have an umbrella or raincoat with us. We know all about Sod's law, so we shouldn't blame these things for ruining our day. Yet most of us do, much of the time.

Consequently, everyday living can be very frustrating ... but only if we let it. If we get mad every time we're ambushed by life's little (or big) surprises, we'll be Mr, Mrs or Ms Angry virtually non-stop. We won't be nice people to know and, in all probability, we won't even like ourselves that much.

How to be Calmer, Happier and More Successful

This chapter will give you some easy techniques to help you become calmer, happier and more successful. Sometimes you've got to be prepared simply to accept what happens to you as a done deal, even though it might sound like a bit of a cop-out. Exactly the same applies to things that you have done in the past. When you did them, you had a choice and might have been able to respond differently; but now they're done, dusted and probably can't be undone. You might have told somebody something that, in retrospect, you wish you hadn't, or told them something in the wrong way. But what's done is done. Others will have reacted to an event you created, and the world will have changed for better or worse.

I cannot stress strongly enough that you must allow yourself – or teach yourself – to see the reality staring you in the face, rather than wishing circumstances could be otherwise. Once you are able to accept that things are as they are, you can react to them relevantly. After all, it's utterly pointless to react to something that doesn't exist!

Work towards the Best Outcome

So, events cannot be changed. They happen to you and are out of your control. But your reaction to what happens is absolutely within your power. And how you respond to something that happens determines what the outcome will be for you and those around you. React badly, or wrongly, and the outcome will not be the ideal one for the given situation. Your best bet – if you analyse it – is to start at the end and work backwards. That is to say, work out what the best possible outcome might be, **given that what has already happened cannot be changed**.

We don't usually have much time to think things through: events happen ... we react. But what we can try and do is prepare a sort of generic reaction – a way we can react best, in very general terms, to things that happen. We should try and take a deep breath and remain calm, however unfair a situation might seem. Try to stand back and think practically rather than let our emotions take over. If we can accept that 'shit happens', it shouldn't throw us wildly off course and make us behave irrationally.

Say someone cuts you up on the way to work. You might easily lose your temper with them, chase them, overtake them and cut *them* up to 'teach them a lesson'. You'll then continue your adrenalin-fuelled journey, presenting a considerable hazard to other drivers. Perhaps you'll make yourself late, incur the wrath of your boss and, still flustered, start your working day in a foul mood. Far from ideal ...

Or, when you are cut up, you simply shrug your shoulders and have a little chuckle to yourself. You accept that there are thoughtless drivers about, so it doesn't really surprise you that a moron has done something stupid. You don't react badly at all, and continue on your normal journey to work. Secretly you feel quite good about yourself: you are happy with your standard of driving and mature behaviour. Plus you have a titbit to throw into the small-talk pot when you get to work. You are quietly smug again when a colleague says, 'I don't know how you can keep so calm when people do things like that. I'd chase them and punch them on the nose!' You go into an important meeting already feeling confident and in control, perform excellently and receive high praise from your boss. Suddenly, you are flavour of the month. What a great day!

Clearly the latter is the better outcome. So you should, ideally, look to respond to the cutting-up event by behaving in a manner most likely to deliver that outcome. You accept totally that you will encounter the occasional idiot on the road. You are ready for that eventuality, and it doesn't faze you.

It is almost as if we must trust in fate. A really positive person will be able to look at an apparent stroke of bad luck and think, 'That might have been meant to happen – there might be something even better just around the corner.' In fact, I bet most of us can look back on some of our apparent misfortunes and be thankful for 'lucky escapes'. At the time, the traumatic break-up of a passionate relationship, for example, seems like the end of the world. But without it you would never have been happily settled with your long-suffering wife and smashing kids because you wouldn't have been in a position to meet her in the first place! And if you hadn't missed out on the promotion you desperately wanted, you would never have looked elsewhere at precisely the time the perfect job for you was being advertised.

The message is that 'shit *does* happen', but all that means is that your life may change course slightly – and not necessarily for the worse. There's no rule that says misfortune will inevitably follow misfortune, unless you choose to make it yourself! It's up to each of us to accept that, sometimes, we must simply make the best out of a bad job.

Be Happy and Optimistic

Staying happy and optimistic is important if we are to accept life's events and move towards our goals. Most people dismiss this as trite or unrealistic, but remember that expectation becomes reality, and the world and people seem to react according to how we are.

Think about it. How much more do you achieve when you're happy? How energetic do you feel when you're content and optimistic?

Blame looks backwards, and responsibility looks forwards. We can't take responsibility for everything that life throws our way. However, the one thing we can control is how we feel about it. For example, no one can make you feel annoyed unless you allow them to.

Have a think about some difficult situations that you handled particularly well. What frame of mind were you in? You may well have been feeling angry or disappointed but how did you channel these feelings positively to create a good outcome?

Think about people who perform at exceptional levels and make it anyone, from, say, Richard Branson to Kylie Minogue! When you see them speak they are charismatic, energetic and perform brilliantly. Can they possibly feel the same way every time? Surely some mornings they wake up having not slept so well. That same morning they may well argue with a loved one, get riled by the kids and have toothache – but they still go to their place of work and perform! Despite what is happening around them, they are able to accept the imperfection of events, and rely on responding correctly.

Choose Optimistic Friends

An essential part of feeling good and developing and maintaining an attitude of optimism and happiness is to be with people who create those feelings in you. It is important to limit your time with moaners and whiners.

We tend to attract people according to how we are. Have you noticed how successful people hang out with successful people? Unhappy and pessimistic people hang out with people who are the same.

'Isn't the world terrible?'

'Yes it is. I like you, you agree with me!'

It is difficult to remain optimistic and happy when you're constantly with someone who is glum and negative about themselves and the world. There is always something attractive about someone who presents themselves as upbeat, energetic and forward thinking. Think how it makes you feel when you are with someone who is dynamic, self assured and enthusiastic.

When you are hanging out with someone who is achieving their goals and has the attitude of success, you'll notice that they talk the language of ideas and creativity. They look forwards and speak of opportunities. They have a passion and energy that fuels the conversation. They are enthusiastic about the possibilities and open minded about the outcomes. And you know what? You can become one of them ... now!

It is important to be the thing you wish to become. Therefore, you can start talking in the way I've described even if you don't perceive yourself to be successful. You can act out the traits of successful people. You see, we can all fool ourselves into anything. Unfortunately, most of us fool ourselves into believing that we are not very good at all sorts of things. We use our imagination to conjure up all sorts of pictures of failures and failings. However, what we can imagine vividly we can believe and physically manifest.

Inspire Yourself!

Start pretending to yourself you are exactly as you wish to be, and watch yourself grow into what is acted out. It may help to inspire yourself by finding out more about successful people you admire. Read biographies of people who have achieved greatness; celebrate other people's success and understand what they've done to gain it. Every day we see or hear of ordinary people doing extraordinary things. Read magazines, listen to CDs, watch programmes or films that inspire and motivate you. Invest in creating the climate for success. Create the environment in which you feel it's easiest to act out the role of one of life's winners.

EDDY'S STORY

An old friend, Jenks, called me recently to say that his son, whom I'd known since he was six or seven years old, had got the exam grades he needed to get his first choice of university. Not quite what I was expecting after the last time we'd talked about young Eddy. Then, Jenks was not exactly depressed about his son's performance, but was certainly brutally realistic.

He was pleased that all the exams were finished, but wasn't that optimistic about Eddy's likely results: 'Don't hold your breath' was the gist of it. From what Eddy had said, he'd messed things up, apparently. Stuff like not answering the right questions, and picking the wrong topics to revise. He'd worked hard enough, Jenks graciously admitted, but it sounded like he'd had a bit of 'brain fade' when it came to the crunch. He was pretty sure that they'd be looking at Plan B come September …

I tried to steer the conversation into more optimistic territory, telling him that people frequently reckon they've cocked things up straight after an exam and, most of the time, it's not half as bad as they think. I urged Jenks not to be too hard on his son: 'I bet he does okay.' He was far from convinced.

Pointing out, perhaps unnecessarily, that it was too late to change anything – that the deed had now been done and the die cast – I'd asked about Plan B. What was it? The truth was, they didn't actually have one, as everything had seemed to be going smoothly. Eddy had had a genuine focus and commitment to achieving this goal for himself, so it wasn't a case of parental expectations and pressure causing problems. We were both aware how potent these could be! Jenks had told me several times how he had virtually dropped out of his own 'A' levels because he didn't think he would get the marks his parents were clearly expecting. According to him, he would rather miss the exams altogether than run any risk of letting people – and himself – down. That's what parental expectations can do. But I knew the family well and was sure that they wouldn't have heaped this sort of pressure on Eddy, so I genuinely sympathised with Jenks. I also knew that all they had ever wanted was to provide the support, encouragement and financial backing to at least give Eddy the chance to go to university if that's what he wanted.

I wondered how Jenks would respond over the coming weeks. I'd always known him to be reasonably laid back and philosophical about life, but he was pretty downcast. But, I told him, he didn't actually *know* anything concrete yet, so there was no point in crossing too many bridges. After all, there had to be a chance that everyone fouled up. He'd just have to wait and see. To be fair, he'd fundamentally agreed with me, but was still tending to look on the black side. He knew that it wouldn't be the end of the world if Eddy didn't make it to university, but that they'd set their sights 'a bit higher than a job at Pizzaland ...' I just hoped that he would keep the family's spirits up and that they wouldn't all be wallowing in recriminations and depression for the next few weeks.

I needn't have worried. As I said at the start, when we spoke again, Eddy had been offered his place at university. He never got the grades they'd asked for, as Jenks had suspected – he didn't even get them for his second choice university. But that didn't matter. Obviously the exams *had* been tough for everyone, and he was still offered his preferred option. So crisis averted – well, it just never happened, did it? They had imagined it would, but that's all it was – Jenks's vivid imagination. At least nobody panicked, though, and the family had a relatively decent summer. Unfortunately, the next time I talked to Jenks, more problems were looming.

As soon as I got on to the subject of Eddy being about to fly the nest, I hit the rocks. They were struggling to find him somewhere to live and, quite naturally, none of the family wanted Eddy to be homeless or looking for digs on his own in a strange city. Jenks even suggested that he might not go to university at all.

Hang on, I thought. Weren't all first-year students offered a place in halls of residence these days? It transpired that, yes, they were – providing that they applied for that place at the right time. That, it appeared, had been way before the exams had even started. Jenks, his wife and Eddy had all missed some vital information that was tucked away in the depths of a brochure ... until very recently. As soon as they received the offer of a place, Jenks had chased them up for information about accommodation. 'Oh dear,' said the helpful girl on the phone, 'you missed the deadline, and we have no more places available. I'll send you a leaflet.'

This happened just one week before Eddy was supposed to go away, so I could understand Jenks's pessimism. But I sensed a change in his attitude as our conversation continued. He said that he was making a huge effort not to jump the gun, and that he expected everything to work out as long as they all remained calm and focused. He had worked out a timetable of things to do, and was following it. This was good to hear. He told me there was one possible glimmer of hope in the overall gloom, but that they had heard nothing yet, and were apparently unable to get in contact with anything other than an answering machine.

The leaflet that the girl in the accommodation office had sent them was about a new private development that had been purpose-built for students in the summer. Within minutes of reading it, Jenks had taken the plunge: he'd applied online, and paid a hefty deposit with his credit card. His deposit had been accepted, but that was all they knew. Did that mean a room was now guaranteed? The answering machine was of zero assistance! 'It's a nightmare, Jamil – I'll give it a couple more days, then try and ring again.'

With just three days to go, Jenks called to say that Eddy had got a place in one of the last two student flats available. Amazingly, the place had a commercial gym as part of the basement – sauna, pool, hi-tech equipment, the lot – and the last few student applicants got free membership! Eddy was in a mixed, self-catering, non-smoking flat for five. It was pretty much just as he'd wanted, except that it wasn't on the main campus, but it did have digital television and internet connections in every room. Talk about falling in the sewage plant and coming up smelling of roses, I thought.

I was delighted for them all, and couldn't resist making the observation that if Jenks had sat there cursing his bad luck for just one day longer, Eddy probably wouldn't have been at university at all. He had to agree that I was right – something that gave him much pain! Jenks said that Eddy still grumbled about not being on campus. However, only the other day, even this resolved itself.

Eddy himself called me to let me know how things were going. He had apparently been out to some party at the Students' Union and couldn't make it back to his place (for whatever reason – I hesitated to ask!) A friend had let him crash on cushions on the floor of their room on campus, in one of the halls of residence he'd so badly wanted to be in. And the room was, in his own words, 'crap'! 'What a dive – makes mine look like a five-star hotel,' he continued. When I asked if he'd told his dad about this yet, Eddy said he hadn't, he thought he'd let him stew a bit longer! Clearly he was learning fast and, I'm delighted to say, he hasn't looked back.

Eddy's Experience

We have all had things not work out for us, but we're not born perfect, and will not die perfect. Success does not come from always making the right decision or things always working out as you wish. Although Eddy was disappointed that he didn't get his original wish, the alternative turned out better. We all have examples of things not going to plan but it working out anyway. Maybe we're just good at forgetting that the original plan was not the one that's now making us happy. The uninitiated call it luck, but I bet it's about attitude if you look back at how you handled your disappointment.

Look back over the things that are currently making you happy. How did nature conspire to cock it up by getting in the way of your original choices? What was your attitude and outlook, and how did you end up with the better alternative?

What isn't working out at the moment? Take a good look at some stuff that may fall through at the moment. If it doesn't work out, what might be the better alternatives? You may be surprised what you think of or you may use this to understand the real reasons why you want something, which in turn allows you to think of other options.

Life has dealt us all blows. When you hear or read about someone successful, look for the adversity or challenge they have had to face. Every day we are hearing about or seeing ordinary people achieve extraordinary things, each of these people naturally experiencing the same trauma, incidents and accidents that we all face throughout our lives.

Change Your Reactions

Okay, we know that we all encounter many disappointments and irritations in the course of our average week. They can't be helped – they happen – but it is our own responses to them that transform them into annoyances. After all, if we actually quite liked getting cut up in the car on the school run, it could no longer be called an annoyance! So, let's get real. Let's try and alter our immediate responses to these situations.

Maybe you're a teacher, and what bothers you is the kids running in the corridor. Or maybe it *is* getting cut up in the car on the way to work. Whatever your particular gripe, let's not expect these annoyances to just stop!

What I want you to do is decide how many times you will allow these things to happen before you get upset about them. Let's say you have a 15-minute drive to work, and you establish that you will usually get cut up by bad drivers three times in that journey. Make a mental tally of three bad drivers that you will tolerate, and tick them off. Then, by all means, feel free to shout and swear at the fourth one you encounter!

By doing this you will be experiencing the powerful idea that you can control your emotions – perhaps the one true power we've all got. You will never control the actions of others, of nature, fate or God, but you can control how you react to them. Our only chance of changing our outer world is to change our inner world.

A friend of mine used to get intensely annoyed when listening to the radio and hearing journalists putting words into people's mouths. The expression 'So what you're saying is ...' would send him apoplectic! Similarly, he'd get annoyed when someone being interviewed was asked an 'off-topic' question by a journalist, and gave an answer simply not to appear rude. The question 'Do you think that David Beckham should be allowed to win his 100th cap for England?' asked, let's say, to the Prime Minister, might have elicited a response of, 'Well, if I was manager, probably not. But I'm not in charge, and it's really none of my business.' Then, suddenly – in the next news headlines – my friend would hear: 'Prime Minister urges England to drop Beckham!', as if the PM had specifically gone on air to make a statement about it.

As this would happen with alarming regularity, and radios were frequently getting broken in his house, my friend decided to make a note of all these instances and report back to his mates on a weekly basis. It became a sort of game, to see who could spot the most – a bit like 'I spy' on a long car journey. That way such annoyances actually became sources of entertainment rather than irritation.

Someone else I know used to get extremely irritated by her neighbour's burglar alarm going off during the day when he was at work. Sheila would hear this incessant, piercing, electronic 'whooping' several times a week, always, it seemed, when she was trying to get her baby off to sleep in the afternoon. When her husband returned from work in the evening, her sole topic of conversation – for months – would be Bill's damned burglar alarm! Her husband got pretty fed up with this, and suggested she make a note of every time the thing went off, thinking that then he could actually challenge Bill with some concrete evidence, rather than just passing on his wife's general moans about it. He had done this once before, but all Bill had said was, 'Yeah, I know it goes off once in a blue moon but I'm sure it's not that bad.' By itemising dates and times, Sheila felt she was actually doing something proactive about the situation rather than just getting annoyed. After another month, they both confronted Bill about his alarm … with a long and detailed list! He didn't have a leg to stand on and grudgingly agreed to have the alarm looked at. Problem solved.

Dealing with a Crisis

All well and good, but how do you deal with life's real blows, like when someone close to you dies? Can this technique help at all in a genuine personal crisis? I would say yes, it can. The thing is, when we suffer a bereavement there are just so many thoughts and emotions flying around inside our heads that we can easily end up wallowing in a swamp of general sadness and misery. It seems almost impossible to start dealing with our grief because it seems so general, all-encompassing and vague. Now it might sound trite and simple, but the best way to tackle big subjects – as will become clear many times throughout this book – is to break them down into easily manageable chunks.

So get out a sheet of paper, and start writing down a series of individual wishes and thoughts. Things about the situation that make you angry or sad. Things you perhaps wish you had done. Then tackle them, one by one. You might wish you had made that last trip to see your mum in time – that might be a source of real angst for you. But break it down: neither of you knew that she was going to die then. These things happen when we least expect them. Would she have held it against you? Probably not. So don't beat yourself up about it. Tick it off your list and move on to the next issue. You have dealt with one aspect; now handle the rest in the same way. By being proactive and confronting your worries, you are regaining control of your life. It really does work.

Whatever else you do, it is really important to try and be proactive rather than just reactive. We feel at our lowest and most powerless when things are out of our hands, but that is usually because we allow our instinctive emotions to take control. As soon as we begin to exert some influence over them, things start to improve. When you think about it, making a list really isn't that hard to do!

Points to Remember

- **There are many things in life you can't control.** Your emotions you can. You are responsible for how you feel at any and every given time.

- **Happiness is not dependent on anything.** Look at the television and you will see people in less fortunate circumstances than most and you know what? They can still do happiness! You can choose to be happy now. Start smiling when you reach the full stop at the end of this sentence.
- **Success is not about having good or bad things happen to you** – it will only ever be about how you react to both.
- **It is easy to fight when you are winning.** True character and attitude is most noticeable when times are tough.

CHAPTER 7

Build the Perfect You

OUR SELF-ESTEEM – or self-image – is our perception of our own worth. The critical thing to remember here is that word 'perception'. When those of us with a poor self-image look at ourselves, it's a bit like walking through the hall of mirrors in a fairground. The distorted reflection we see is what we think we are, as we are unable to fully appreciate things as they really are. Our perception of what we are is our own guess at how other people think of us, or how we match up to all sorts of bizarre yardsticks we set for ourselves.

I'm sure you've heard people use the phrase 'it's just the way I am' when justifying their behaviours and actions, and we all nod with acceptance. Perhaps you've used the expression yourself. But this statement simply isn't true. We are not born with our behaviour patterns. We are taught them.

Do you catch yourself saying things like, 'Of course I've got a temper, it's the red hair'? 'Of course I get angry, my granddad had a right temper'? 'Of course I'm fun-loving, I'm half-Irish'? Well, if you do, you're talking nonsense! There are no genes that equate to any of these traits, so you can't blame them on anything or anyone else!

Take the way we tend to compare ourselves physically with other people. Well, to be strictly accurate, what we actually do is compare ourselves with society's ideals as seen in adverts, movies and fashion houses. Then we compare other people with those ideals, and see by how much each of us differs. If you have a poor self-image, you will notice other people's strong points, and conclude that you are inferior.

Make the Best of What You Are

In an ideal world, you would see yourself as you really are and not make judgements about it. You may be shorter than average, but instead of wishing you were taller, you would positively identify all the benefits you gain from being short. These might include having a better sense of balance, or a reduced risk of developing back problems. Or it may be realising that you are not on your own, and that you might have a better chance than someone taller of getting together with a fantastic man who is also on the short side.

You might also have the awareness and intelligence to accept that there is nothing you can do to change the situation. If you were not born with tall genes, that's it – fact – you won't actually become tall. Rather than denying your lack of altitude or trying to cover it up with massively built-up shoes or secret under-trouser stilts, you accept it and make the best of what you are. Just because you are – physically – what you are doesn't make you any better or worse as a person than someone else with entirely different physical characteristics.

Modern society doesn't help. Clothes and other products are, inevitably, geared towards the average. Extra tall, fat, thin or short people tend to be marginalised and have less choice. Advertisements feature models who are best equipped to show off the product. Clothing hangs better on tall, skinny girls, and blokes that hang better are more likely to be chosen to show off Lycra swimming trunks. Their facial features will be as near perfectly proportioned as science can measure (but, again, that makes them far from average as very few of us are that perfect). The thing is, if you can accept yourself for what you are you will be much happier in your own skin.

In other words, it's pointless moaning about what you haven't been born with, be it a physical characteristic or a talent. Equally, it's important to appreciate the gifts nature *has* given you. Then what you must do is go out and make the very best of the cards you have been dealt!

Don't Measure Your Value in Terms of Achievements

We tend to value ourselves solely by our achievements. Many people with low self-esteem are able to measure themselves only by how much they earn; how 'important' a position they hold at work; how many committees they are on; how fast or flashy a car they drive; how much they spend on this, that or the other. They let other people know these details because they assume everyone else will think the same way and be dutifully impressed. Such individuals might appear confident and happy but, deep down, they are terrified that when they stop 'achieving' they will be found out as fundamentally insubstantial people.

If this is you, what happens if you lose your job? What happens when the money dries up and you become less important? Quite simply, you would have nothing to fall back on, and – in your own eyes – would become an instant failure. In our ideal world, you would be able to see yourself as intrinsically valuable, worth something just for being the person you are: decent, thoughtful, considerate, kind, gener-ous and supportive of others. Think like this and you can begin to like yourself – really, honestly, genuinely – without feeling you need to engage in 'dog-eat-dog' battles for the key to the executive toilet and desperate bids for approval through position and possessions.

Don't Expect Everybody to Like You

Look at how we want everybody to like us. Big mistake. We are all different, and there are people we were simply never designed to like! If you spend all your time trying to ensure that everyone likes you, you end up not having the chance to be yourself. You try so hard to either 'fit in' with things that really don't interest you, or to agree with stuff you honestly don't have any feelings for. It's important for others to see us for what we genuinely are, because that's the only way we get honest, relevant feedback from them about ourselves. If we pretend all the time – just to please – any feedback is completely misleading. And, of course, feedback from others has a huge influence on how we perceive ourselves.

The way we are perceived by our family can have a big impact on our lives. How influenced would you say you've been all your life by those closest to you, your immediate family? You must remember, however, that they have also responded to how they see you. You may never have got praise from your mother because she thought you didn't need it, mistaking the way you mask your insecurity with false confidence for real confidence. This scenario, in turn, may contribute to an increasing lack of confidence as you see the praise lavished elsewhere. I'm not saying this is always the case. Some people may not be responding just to how they see you – they may be responding to how they are. They may be treating you in a particular way because of their own fears, insecurities, prejudices or jealousies. This may not even be personal; it may just be a generalisation about the clothes you wear, the job you do or how they perceive your partner or friends. However, we are never really able to see ourselves through the eyes of others.

Don't Rely on the Opinions of Others

Don't automatically assume, either, that someone else's opinion has more 'clout' than yours. Those with low self-esteem will keep trying to change according to what others say, without thinking rationally: 'Hey, what if I'm right and so-and-so's wrong?' In our ideal world, that should be your default thinking. Don't rule out someone else's views, but balance them. Consider them. If they sound like a load of rubbish, or seem heavily laden with ulterior motives, quietly set them to one side for 'binning'! You don't have to do it aggressively – just positively, in your own mind.

Be Yourself

What is paramount for your self-worth is to be happy being yourself. It is when you start trying to be someone you're not that the trouble starts. It's daft, but we've all done it. If someone doesn't like you, that's up to them, and it really shouldn't bother you too much. However, if what they dislike is a mask, and not the real you, that's not fair. You are not being fair on yourself. Actually, you're not being fair on anyone else, either, because it gives them faulty feedback. You might think, for example, that you are lousy at establishing relationships when sober, so every time you are in a position to socialise, you try and become someone successful … powered by alcohol. But you always overdo it a bit, and people don't like that 'someone successful' because he is always drunk. Unfortunately, you'll find – and we all do – that we're not very good at being someone else. The mask will slip at some point, and we always fear for when it might. So we try far too hard. Familiar tale? Judy Garland, for all her lack of self-esteem, had it spot on when she said: 'Always be a first-rate version of yourself instead of a second-rate version of somebody else.'

It's massively important to appreciate that, in 99 out of 100 cases, our perception is faulty. Not in everything, but it's a pretty safe bet that we all have our blind spots. Everybody jumps to conclusions based on dodgy suppositions in some aspect or other of life. Just think what that might mean to how we carry on, day to day. Living life according to misleading information creates untold and largely unnecessary misery all over the place! You owe it to yourself to accept the 'you' that is real, and to make the very best you can of it. What I can do – and it truly isn't that hard – is to help you make the 'perfect you' (or as near as we can get!)

How to Get On with Other People

Almost all of what you achieve in life will be a direct result of how you get on with other people. It is important to practise enthusiastic self-praise, for it is how you think and feel which determines the quality and tone of your communication with others.

Notice how often you talk to yourself – it really is almost

all of the time. It is very rare for us to have a 'quiet mind'. What things are you saying that affect your self-image?

> 'Traffic! Great! I'm going to turn up to work raging again.'
>
> 'I'm always late. I can never do anything right.'
>
> 'It's another bad hair day. Great! I'll just turn up at the meeting looking like a tramp.'
>
> 'Why is life so complicated for me?'

Working with top performers in their respective fields, I've noticed that their success seems to be simply an expression of themselves. I encourage everyone I work with to treat their work as an opportunity for self-expression. When you think of people like Richard Branson, Ian Botham, Stelios and Anita Roddick, they seem to have run their business or played their sport in line with their personality. When you are at work or playing sport, do you go about it according to who you *really* are, or does it compromise you?

Understand your self-image. This in itself will not allow you to have new abilities, but it will point you in the direction of maximising your existing attributes and assets. Once you have seen the real you, accept yourself. No one is perfect, and sometimes our unique talent lies within the area that we may perceive as a weakness. Is your chaotic mind really a creative one? Maybe being quiet shows your ability to be considerate and thoughtful, allowing you to develop into a person looked upon as the voice of reason, free from egotistical, rash or emotional decision making.

You can probably think now of something you perceive as a flaw or a weakness in your personality. If you explore your past, however, I bet you could think of a time or a task where that flaw worked in your favour, and turned out to be a strength. Allow success to be an expression of yourself.

SIMON'S STORY

An old friend and I used to catch up with each other every few weeks or so in a superb Victorian pub next to the railway station. It always had great real ales, excellent wines and whiskies and delicious food. Unfortunately, on this particular occasion – as I was about to discover – it also had Simon Bacon. I hadn't yet met him, but Mark, my friend, had just spotted him up at the bar and apologised to me in advance. He doubted we would be able to escape getting 'Baconed', explaining that this bloke – a salesman – could be 'a bit of an arse', especially if he had just pulled off another of his 'mega' deals.

That was all we needed. I thought we'd come for a nice quiet pint. I asked if there wasn't any way Mark could 'deflect' him. The answer, it seemed, was in the negative. As Simon Bacon approached, Mark leant towards me conspiratorially and whispered hurriedly that he was okay really but that, unfortunately, the true Simon was extremely well hidden. He said that Simon had fingers in lots of pies and did him a few favours, so it was best not to upset him. He promised to find us of a way of escaping in a bit, and urged me to remember that although Simon might well come over as racist, sexist and crass, he didn't mean anything by it. Mark described him as ignorant, rather than malicious. Bizarrely, Mark added that he was Jewish, which seemed irrelevant until I considered the inaptitude of someone Jewish being saddled with the name 'Bacon'.

Simon Bacon certainly looked the part of the salesman. Although small and on the chubby side, he was expensively dressed and loaded with 'bling': gold rings, Rolex watch, sharp suit, long overcoat and lashings of upmarket aftershave.

As Simon hailed Mark – 'Well, well, well, if it isn't young Sedgley! How's it hanging, sunshine?' – I was becoming more intrigued than annoyed at the prospect of the inevitable interruption. Mark put on a pretty good show of pretending to be pleased to see him, exchanging healthy banter regarding what he called the 'murky world of property', and asking if Simon had been starring on the *Watchdog* consumer television show again. It was a bit like asking someone when they were last on *Crimewatch*! Mark was actually remarkably convincing.

Simon took it on the chin, replying almost as if he'd rehearsed the lines many times before. He said that someone had to do it, and that no one did it better than 'Simey B'. He sat down with us, assuming that we wouldn't mind, and asked who I was while extending his hand of friendship for a firm shake. 'Simon Bacon, sales consultant,' he said breezily.

With me still somewhat lost for words, Mark told him that I was Jamil, hypnotist. That threw him momentarily, as he said he was expecting Mark to say 'snake charmer'. Next he started going on about only weak, under-confident people being susceptible to hypnosis, and that I would never be able to hypnotise him. 'Perish the thought!' I said to myself. At this point Mark jumped in to explain that Simon had a bit of a self-confidence problem. Far too much of it for his own good, it appeared. 'Can't have too much self-esteem, that's what I was always told. Always gotta be one step ahead or the bastards'll try and stuff you.'

When I politely enquired as to the identity of these bastards, Simon launched into a list as long as his arm, including bank managers, health and safety 'bastards', the Inland Revenue and everyone else in the sales prevention business. He insisted they hated him because he was so much more successful than they. He said that he'd never had it easy – always had to fight snobs like that 'tooth and claw'. And now – just because he'd got a Bentley and a big house – they thought that he owed them something. I was sure that he probably did, but asked anyway, out of politeness. Simon roared back that he owed nobody anything, asking whose round it was and looking intently at poor Mark. I quickly realised that this wasn't a question and, with a reluctant sigh of acceptance, Mark disappeared up to the bar.

Simon leant towards me, slightly shiftily, and confided that he was into something 'rather tasty' but 'very hush-hush'. Something, he thought, that with my contacts (who did he think I was?!) I might be able to make some money out of, adding that a friend of Mark's was a friend of his 'and all that'. Again, out of politeness, I raised my eyebrows in feigned interest. He expanded on his scheme. Said it was to do with property finance, that he'd worked it all out, business plan and everything, and that there were millions in it. He reckoned that he'd 'got a bloke out in Greece' on the inside, setting up deals, then he'd walk in, blow them away and they'd just lie back to have their tummies tickled! His turn of phrase was punchy and colourful. He said that he didn't take prisoners, and that if I put any timeshare business his way, there was a 'big drink' in it for me.

Just then, Mark returned with three pints of foaming ale. Simon, looking ostentatiously at his hugely expensive watch, gasped. Cursing, he exclaimed that he had to see a business colleague in town in 20 minutes. It was a very important meeting, and he was sorry, but he had to dash. Adding that it had been nice meeting me, he gulped down his free pint and bustled importantly towards the door. Then he was gone. Yes, he was a bit of an arse – Mark was quite right – and quite a contrast to the last bloke he'd introduced me to in that pub.

I hoped I had seemed suitably impressed, and asked Mark where was the old boy we had met the last time we were in there. 'Walter, wasn't it? He was great – I really enjoyed talking to him. I thought you said he was always here?' The previous time we'd met up, the pub was nearly full. There were two spare seats around a table in the corner, but an old man was sitting there on his own with a newspaper. Mark seemed to know him, though, and suggested we went over. Walter was only too pleased for us to do so. Never once during our evening did he enter the conversation without being asked – he just sat quietly, enjoying a couple of pints, from time to time acknowledging people with a cheery smile and a wave of his hand.

He was clean and tidy – well dressed without being showy. Didn't seem exactly on the pensioners' poverty line, either, as he insisted on buying both of us a drink when he visited the bar. When it came to our rounds, he declined on both occasions with polite thanks. Whenever he did speak, he gave the impression of being extraordinarily wise. Mark said later that everybody in the place had time for him, and that he never had a bad word to say about anyone – always managed to see people's strengths rather than their weaknesses. At least, that's all he would comment upon. He spoke his mind in a gentle but firm sort of way, and I'd gained the impression that, although old, he wouldn't allow himself to be pushed around. Anyway, this time he wasn't there.

Yes, remembered Mark, it was Walter, and it was a sad story. He had apparently died about three weeks previously. No fuss. Everyone had thought he was dozing in the corner. He had a little smile on his face but that was it – he'd supped his last pint. 'But you know the amazing thing?'

I would do very shortly. Mark continued that a few of the pub regulars had thought it only right to represent the pub at the funeral. He observed that there's nothing worse than hearing of just one man and his dog 'seeing someone off'. So six of them had gone along ... and couldn't get in. There wasn't room in the church! Walter had left money for a slap-up wake in the Commodore (a nearby hotel) afterwards, and that's when Mark had found out ...

Mark paused, smiled, and shook his head as if still in bewilderment. It seemed that old Walter had been a leading heart surgeon, top of the tree. He'd made a fortune on the stock market in his younger days on some gold-mining shares that shot up suddenly. He'd given thousands to charity over the years. And he'd won the Military Cross at the Battle of the Somme. And nobody in the pub had known a thing about it ... they never had an inkling.

I particularly remembered how relaxed he had seemed when I'd met him that one time, as if he had nothing to prove to anyone. What a fantastic feeling that must have been. At that moment, Simon Bacon dashed back in, apparently having forgotten to mention something to Mark. The contrast could hardly have been more vivid.

Simon's Experience

We all know someone like Simon. They simply decide to wear their personality. Is the real Simon made up of the words he uses and the watch he wears, or is it really masked beneath them? Self-image cannot be worn. It is not about personality – although that can be an expression of it – it is about character. It is all about what we stand for and who we intrinsically are. It is the fundamentals of what we say and do, as all our behaviours result from our thoughts.

Get to Know Yourself

Think about a celebrity you see on television or in the paper. Imagine yourself in their situation, good or bad. How would you improve it?

Imagine you had their fame, money and lifestyle – but your own thoughts. Play around with having a set of different circumstances or being in a different situation, but see how your morals, values and ideas would make you deal with it. Play out the celeb's life and see how you could improve it simply by being you, but with different resources.

This fun exercise allows you to get to know yourself better. By seeing yourself with a different set of circumstances you get to play around with your outside world and see how much of your inside world stays the same. Would money change you? Or would you like to have it so you could give it away? What would you do if your once-famous career was in tatters after that very public scandal? Some of your principles and values may stay the same no matter how many times you play this game, but some may change. Note the consistencies within your thoughts and decision making, as these make up your core values.

Whatever you end up finding out about yourself is fine. The key to improving your self-image lies in self-acceptance. For you must accept that whatever makes you tick is already enough for you to gain significantly more success. You may already spend a lot of time feeling bad about attributes you haven't got, or would like to have, but self-acceptance is about celebrating what is good about you. Do this and it will multiply, and you know what? The other stuff you don't like about yourself will change anyway, simply by feeling great about your strengths.

Every day, you do fantastic things – you just don't realise it. Today, you will probably do things that some of the most successful people on the planet are not capable of doing – it might be something to do with the children, an ill relative or a difficult situation that is thrust upon you. Start to feel good about the things you do and who you are. There is no one like you, and your very special purpose on this earth will reveal itself to you.

Points to Remember

- **You look in the mirror and what do you see?** Try to see right through you. If you were transparent, what qualities would be coursing through your veins? What qualities would be pumping through your organs? Can you see the words 'loyalty', 'service', 'fun', 'generosity', 'integrity'? What would you like there to be more of?

- **What qualities do you express that make you most happy?** Do you feel most alive when you've put in a hard day's work? Or is it when you've helped a stranger or had fun with a friend?

- **Choose one quality and do it more today.** Thomas Edison patented over a thousand commercial items in his lifetime, yet he only ever worked on one project at a time. Choose one thing you'd like to do more of, and check out the results. Do it for a day, a week or just when you remember, but see if your outer world changes as you transform your inner one.

CHAPTER 8

Trust Yourself

E VERY DAY, WE trust thousands of strangers: the pilots who fly our planes, the engineers who design them, the workers who manufacture them. Most of the time, we trust our doctors and nurses, our police force and even our financial advisors. Okay, we often don't trust politicians, estate agents and people whose eyes are too close together, but you get the general picture.

Trust is vital to effective human understanding and co-operation. For us to be trusting means that we are able to be forgiving and empathetic to others. With trust comes the ability to communicate without prejudice. We all know people who pride themselves on their cynicism. Their first consideration in any interaction with other people – whether individuals or organisations – is 'What's in it for them?' Their default position in life is to distrust the motivations and actions of others. Theirs is a position of total defence: if they don't put their trust in people, they can't get hurt. That trust can't be shattered. They won't ever be disillusioned … again. 'Again' is an important word here, because for somebody to hold such a miserable and negative view of humankind, they must have been hurt by something or someone in their past. After all, they didn't start out cynical:

'Come on son, just one more spoonful of this yummy baby food.'

'Why, Daddy? You're only trying to make me go to sleep and be quiet so you and Mummy can have fun without me. I've got your number … so I won't!'

No, we were born trusting. The great sadness with some people is that – at some point early in life – they were hurt, bullied, manipulated or deserted by those in whom they placed their trust. They became unable to build up their belief and self-esteem and, consequently, unable to take the odd let-down with a mere shrug of the shoulders. They learnt to expect disappointment as a matter of course and so grew a protective, cynical shell to hide behind.

We all know people like this, and although we can frequently see a warm person beyond the 'front', it rarely appears in public. This means that they're very rarely warm and open with others. They're not outgoing, not much fun (though for some of us, watching totally predictable misery is actually quite funny!) and people find it hard to warm to them. Maybe that's you? If it is, there is some good news:

you can learn to trust – and accept the risks of trusting – again. I'll show you how in this chapter.

What is Your Belief System?

As humans, we're very good at finding evidence to fit what we believe. If, for example, I believe that people are untrustworthy and everyone lies, then I look for evidence of this and act in a way that brings this behaviour out in people as a reaction. As a result, I am underlining my own belief system.

What is your belief system?

All parking attendants are unfair.

BMW drivers are rude.

Celebrities do things only for publicity.

Bosses only promote people they are friends with.

Neighbours only like people who keep themselves to themselves.

Can you think of one of your negative beliefs, one that will hold you back? Now think of ways in which you might look for, or even make up, evidence to support it. Most of the information might come from second-hand opinion or hearsay, or ways in which you interpret outcomes and feedback.

Because we always look to prove ourselves right, we need to make sure our beliefs have a good basis in truth, to help us to live our lives successfully. Supporting wrongly held beliefs will not give us a firm foundation for a balanced, confident and therefore happy position in life.

How to Learn to Trust Yourself

What we should really be doing is trusting ourselves. Most people we perceive to be open, friendly and approachable manage this quite naturally.

We should be prepared to trust our own instincts, our intuition. This doesn't mean being naïve – it just means not being instinctively inward-looking and defensive. And when we start to make 'trust' – as opposed to suspicion – our default, the world begins to reflect back to us positively. Others treat us as we treat them. Trust becomes the most solid bond that people can have.

Believe in Your Abilities

The other aspect involved in trusting yourself is that of achievement. Whether or not you believe it right now, all of us have sufficient assets and abilities in our make-up to be able to be successful. By trusting our own instincts, we will inevitably get on better with others. We will make more friends and have more fun, which – I'm sure you'll agree – is a significant benefit. But we will also enjoy more success because part of trusting in ourselves is trusting in our own abilities – those we can lay our hands on right now.

Sure, we can all grow, and should want to develop and improve ourselves. We all have the potential and ability to learn new skills. But these can take time to perfect, and plenty of hard work. But while you're trying to develop any new skills, it is important to remember *not* to get too downhearted or frustrated if they seem hard to acquire. It might appear that the gap between what you have, and what you think you need, is immense ... but don't be fooled! What you have right now, without any additional stuff, will see you through, as long as you focus on it and trust it.

We are all far more talented than we think we are. We all have a far more comprehensive built-in skill set than we imagine. The thing to do – and it's not that hard – is to take a good, long look at yourself. Don't worry about being bigheaded (you're talking to yourself about all this, remember!) Just make an inventory of your skills, what you're good at – socially, at work, in sport and leisure. Then try and focus on these strengths, and polish them, day by day. You might be good at making people around you feel happy ... when you can be bothered. Well try and be bothered just a little more often! Make a tiny bit more effort and you'll reap the rewards. You'll notice how people enjoy your company more which, naturally, makes you feel better. All positive feedback does.

I'll give you a few concrete examples. Take the hugely successful rock band Status Quo. No one has ever pretended (least of all Quo themselves) that this band has been at the cutting edge of musical development. They've never pushed any frontiers. What they have done – brilliantly, in my opinion – is honed their knack of arranging three basic chords – just three – in such a way that they sound ever-so-slightly different with each new song. They hit upon a successful formula many years ago, and polished it until it gleamed. They focused on what they were best at, and squeezed every last drop of success from that ability.

In sport, there was Kevin Keegan – a footballer who became world renowned. Yet Keegan was never blessed with half the natural ability of many of his peers. He simply worked hard at perfecting the talents he actually possessed. In cricket, Geoff Boycott did the same. History might suggest that both were massive talents in their respective fields, yet in truth their talent was nothing extraordinary. Sure, they became extremely good at certain things. But, most of all, they were extremely good at identifying and accepting their limited strengths, and polishing them until they sparkled. They refused to be frustrated by not being fantastic at everything, or finding certain knacks hard to acquire. They trusted that the tools they naturally possessed could make them succeed. You should try it!

Identify just a few of your key strengths or qualities. It might be your ability to listen, to negotiate, or just that you're very good with numbers. Imagine if you relied on these skills to get everything you wanted. They have already contributed to your success, but imagine if you could polish them into being 20 per cent better. Think about how your life would be in 10 years' time if, from this moment, you lived every day using these star qualities. After all, these are things you are already good at, and it's easier to take something from good to great than from bad to good.

ELLEN'S STORY

I was having a quiet drink with an old girlfriend. Well, she was a friend and she was a girl, and we had always got on really well – as friends – from our college days. Ellen was having a few problems in meeting someone – anyone – that she might be able to build a long-term relationship with. On reflection, that sounds rather too desperate. It was just that she did like having a man around, and her job and social circumstances made it hard for her to meet anyone new.

Bravely (as she was, and still is, a feisty lady), I suggested that she might try an online dating website. Bad idea, apparently! She exploded, saying that it made her sound like some sad, desperate, middle-aged loser who couldn't find herself a man. Still I ploughed on regardless, reminding her that, actually, she couldn't – she hadn't been out on a date for ages. Did I have a death wish? There's a great old saying that once you realise you're in a hole, stop digging. However, I thought I could save things with a bit of charm, and told her that although she might be 40, she was still a beautiful woman, and that there was no reason on earth why …

Help! Even as I said this, I felt myself unable to suppress a smile, which Ellen instantly picked up on. She obviously thought I was taking the mickey, which – honestly – I wasn't. It was just that the way those words came out sounded like a line from some tacky chick-flick. The trouble is it was exactly what I had meant to say – it just sounded naff.

She honestly did have so much going for her, and I was amazed that she couldn't see it.

Still smarting, she said that if she'd got so much going for her, how come she hadn't been out on a date in two years? I suggested that she just didn't go to the right places where she'd be likely to meet the sort of person she'd be interested in, and vice versa. It's not an unusual state of affairs – after all, she had a son aged 11 and was a barrister. She couldn't exactly drop into her local pub or, worse still in her opinion, go out clubbing, because she'd grown out of all that. But there are plenty of people in the same boat, as I told her. Thankfully, it's never happened to me, but it's something more and more people have to face up to these days, especially with divorce rates being so much higher than in the past. More to the point, she continued, she had grown out of dating. She explained that you know what to do when you're single – properly single. But that once you've met Mr Right – or, in her case, Mr Wrong – it's game over. You don't need to keep look-ing, so you get out of the habit – out of practice. What she was saying seemed to make a lot of sense.

So while I could clearly see Ellen's difficulty, I could equally see that nothing would change unless she made something happen. And she obviously wasn't happy on her own. I asked her what was really so bad about trying the internet. I mean, it's no different from a lonely hearts – sorry, contact – column in the local rag, is it? That was exactly her point. She then let me into a little secret – that she had tried the local rag a few months after she and Piers had split up. Apparently it was a total disaster. Total! It turned out that the first bloke she had met was dead nervous and full of Dutch courage – in Ellen's words, 'drunk as a skunk'.

But she did give it another go, and this time she had known what to look out for. The next guy had actually seemed quite nice – good job, 'GSOH' and quite fit, she said. But he obviously wasn't interested in her, apparently. It had all started off fairly quietly, then fizzled out altogether. Ellen had no intentions of putting herself through that wringer again.

Fair enough, I observed, but maybe if she hadn't gone into the second rendezvous with fixed ideas – courtesy of her 'Oliver Reed' experience – things might have been different. It sounded to me that she just wasn't going to risk giving it a fair go. Her date would have sensed that in no time. Then, when he found he couldn't coax the real Ellen into the open, he would have given up on her ... and I wouldn't have blamed him!

'Thanks, pal!' The lady was far from amused.

I told her that it seemed pretty obvious to me that if you give off a bad vibe, that's what you'll get back. You can't pre-judge everyone – you've got to trust your instincts. If you're bright enough to play the game to begin with, as Ellen undoubtedly was, when and if it starts going pear-shaped, you've got all the social skills needed to knock it on the head. No problem.

Ellen clearly wasn't convinced. She also seemed to have some weird preconceptions about anyone who used the internet. Seemed to think they were all either sex fiends or paedophiles. She said she didn't want to expose herself or her computer to those sorts of risk. As a frequent internet user myself, what did that make me?!

I reassured her that no one would be looking to 'groom' her. I pointed out that if she thought anything was even the slightest bit dodgy, it wasn't rocket science – she just didn't take it any further. The most she was doing was potentially making contact with a stranger and, in a lot of ways, it was much safer doing it 'virtually' than doing it for real. If she was remotely worried she should take a friend along as a chaperone, I concluded.

Ellen let slip a half smile, and reluctantly agreed that her views might sound the tiniest bit prehistoric. I reminded her that she was a very busy person, and that the sort of guys she'd like to meet would be busy people, too – people who wouldn't have the time or, like her, the inclination to do what 20-somethings do to meet a member of the opposite sex. When you think about it logically, quietly browsing the internet in the evening – with a nice bottle of Chablis – is an exceptionally civilised and relaxing way of testing the market. I suggested to her that it could also be a lot of fun! Seriously, she just had to trust that she had the nous to handle it, and I knew for certain that she did.

The next time Ellen and I met up – some six months later – she seemed a whole lot more laid back about things. She had given internet dating a go, and had enjoyed most of the experience. She'd met some extraordinary people, too. One weird bloke had seemed normal enough until, after a couple of glasses of vino, he'd insisted that Ellen look at his 'latest purchase'. It was a pen with a compass and torchlight built in. He'd demonstrated it in ridiculous detail, explaining that it was absolutely perfect for his hobby. The mind boggled! She invited me to hazard a guess, but I really couldn't imagine what it might be. As it transpired, I wouldn't have got it in a million years. He used to go to his local church late at night to practise playing the organ. The torchlight helped him find the church door keyhole in the dark, and he used the pen to make notes on his sheet music. Goodness only knows what the compass was for – it was all too surreal. Apparently he'd play for hours in the lightless loft: 'Bach's organ works,' he'd claimed.

'Good for Bach,' I replied, teasing that he sounded just what Ellen was looking for. She fell for it hook, line and sinker, and said that I had to be joking because this guy had been seriously odd, and that she'd told him so. She couldn't stop laughing, and he'd sheepishly got up and left. Good for Ellen! But then – just as I was beginning to think that Ellen would be forever unlucky in love – she hit me with the pay-off. She had actually met someone through the internet with whom she'd really clicked. A bit of a reformed rogue, she reckoned; a psychiatrist who was, seemingly, a complete nutter out of work. A bit overweight but, she added, 'I'll soon sort that out.' What could she possibly mean, I wondered mischievously?

I detected a genuine gleam in her eye, and suspected that Ellen really fancied this guy. I also suspected that she was in complete control, and confident that she was doing the right thing. What convinced me completely was her asking – out of the blue – whether I'd be a witness at her wedding! I agreed, of course. Ellen married Seve the swarthy psycho five months later and, I'm delighted to say, is now ecstatically happy with life at 41.

Ellen's Experience

If we trust in what we are and what we've got, we can start to maximise it. We become more intuitive and understand 'playing to our strengths'. As soon as we are more relaxed about ourselves, we find it easier to hear those subconscious voices guiding us from within. Not only do we hear them but, more importantly, we truly understand what they are saying too.

If you think of your 'best performances' – this could be at work, in sport or within the family – I can pretty much guarantee that you were not frustrated, anxious or worried when you were doing them. By accepting ourselves, we give ourselves the best opportunity of using our skills to our advantage. Frustration and anxiety will be more damaging then whatever skills you lack.

You may at the moment be willing yourself to find a particular answer to a dilemma, instead of just allowing a more passive process of listening to your feelings to happen. For example, you may wish to buy a new house. If the decision is proving difficult even though it seems like it should be a 'no brainer', something is causing conflict emotionally. The house might be a sound investment and the right price, but is its lack of beauty causing the conflict, as you have a deep-routed need for aesthetics you are trying to ignore? Sometimes struggle and effort simply occur from a conflict between different motivations within the answer to your dilemma.

Find a Solution

Write down several solutions to the same problem on scraps of paper. Mix them up with your eyes closed. Grab one and open it. List what skills you need to make that solution work. Do you have those skills? Do you need to improve them? Do the same with another potential solution to the problem. You'll see a pattern emerging and you'll find that, for some reason, one solution seems so much easier to be enthusiastic about and inspires so many more ideas.

Although the potential solutions may seem different, the skills required to make them work will probably be pretty much the same. You'll also notice that these are skills you have used in similar situations in the past. Maybe think of a course of action that you have taken previously in order to resolve an issue and how the skills that you used were not newly acquired, but were attributes that still lie within you now. You may find yourself gaining confidence by understanding that you have already dealt with situations in the past that you currently believe are new. You'll see that the bulk of the skills you already have are enough to affect the chosen course of action. Go on – prove it to yourself!

Think of an issue you have at the moment. Are your thoughts being clouded by unhelpful information? Perhaps you are being influenced by someone's uninformed opinion. Or are you second guessing some external factor that can never be calculated? Maybe you are listening to hearsay or the opinion of the press, or are imagining what has happened to others in the same predicament.

'People from my family don't go to university.'

'I'm a bit old to be going back to studying.'

'If it doesn't work out, my friends will laugh at me.'

'If I can't do it, I've wasted all that time.'

Allow yourself to evaluate things quickly without the distraction of over-analysis. Sometimes when we weigh things up too carefully we get caught up in information which we believe is relevant but actually is not.

Points to Remember

- **How many times have you performed a small task, it's gone wrong, and you've immediately said, 'I knew I was going to do that!'?** Well, the thing is, you did know. We instinctively know if the coffee cup is stacked precariously on the tray, but we override our instinct to fit what we want to believe. Listen to yourself more, and follow what you intuitively believe.

- **If you do something lots, let's say driving, you just know how to do it.** That is true of anything. Trust that whatever it is, because you have the experience, your subconscious just knows how to do it. You really can fall backwards and know that you will catch yourself.

- **Think now about a problem in your life.** Evaluate it with an instinctive decision. Now, if you were to do that, what would be the best that could happen, and the worst? Now think about it for considerably longer: what's the difference? You'll find very little. It is not time that yields more helpful information; it is our ability to know and trust ourselves in regard to taking appropriate action.

CHAPTER 9

Learn to be Lucky

I T'S UNDOUBTEDLY TRUE that being lucky is not simply a matter of good fortune. Being lucky – or being perceived to be lucky by others – is a result of many things, not the least of which is how we think about life. Those of us who can learn to view things optimistically are far more likely to enjoy good fortune than those who are forever expecting the worst. As we have touched on before, it is something of a self-fulfilling prophecy: if you expect the worst, you usually get it!

The good thing is that you can teach yourself to look on the bright side and, when you keep practising this, life seems to dish out more 'lucky' breaks. It sounds almost too good to be true, I know, but research in the US indicates that you'll live longer, enjoy better relationships, and achieve more at work. In short, you'll be happier.

Expect the Best

Commit to having positive expectations regarding your luck. Be motivated by what you want to happen, not by what you want to avoid.

I'd like you to practise this by going to a party and expecting everyone to like you and be keen to interact with you. The next time you do a presentation, expect everyone to want to listen to what you've got to say.

If you've had a bad experience with a plumber, it doesn't mean you can't expect a better outcome the next time with another. Likewise, the road to work that's always snarled up – just try expecting it not to be.

I'm not saying that you can influence these things. However, with positive expectancy you may find yourself in the frame of mind you want more often, and may bring upon yourself some things that seem to work in your favour – I guess the uninitiated call it luck.

Send Out the Right Signals

What happens to you in life is largely a reflection of what you give out. If you consistently send out negative vibes to the world, you'll simply find that they bounce back at you as your negativity is picked up by those around you. By the same token, if you radiate a positive attitude, you are far more likely to enjoy better 'luck'. Of course, you'll encounter setbacks – everybody does – but with a vibrant, positive attitude you will be resilient enough to dust yourself down and try again.

I've lost count of the number of times that I've tried to help a friend of mine generate more business. A freelance copywriter, he's very bright, clear-thinking and good with people. He has run his own business reasonably successfully for many years, but occasionally he gets mildly depressed that he has not been more successful. In my view, he has been right to think that way for, with his talents, he surely could have achieved a great deal more. His problem has always been one of attitude. It's not that his attitude has been bad – it just could be so much better!

I have constantly encouraged him to make a list of potential new clients, find their telephone numbers and spend a couple of days ringing them up, using his great conversational skills to make these new contacts count in a commercial sense. However, for some inexplicable reason, he has either been afraid to call these numbers altogether, or has given up at the first gentle rejection. He seems to set out with the view that people are all programmed to say 'No, thanks' to his pitch. Then, as soon as one does, he takes it as proof that his negativity is well founded. Amazingly, he totally overlooks the fact that he has actually won several new clients over the years by 'cold-calling' them!

Were he more optimistic in his outlook, he would see each rejection as one step nearer the next winning approach. He would learn from each call he made, identifying any flaws in his 'offer' and fine-tuning it for eventual success. He would also learn that those who said 'No thanks' were not rejecting him as a person: 99 times out of 100 they would have entirely unrelated reasons for not wanting or needing the services he could offer. Unfortunately, he has never seen things in this way and so has tended to give up at the first hurdle.

Need I continue? In my experience, the vast majority of us will be able to empathise completely with my friend's doubts – even those of us who don't seem to show any signs of having them. The good news is that although we have all had such feelings, really successful people understand that it takes only a tiny change in attitude to turn everything around.

Seize Opportunities

You won't find lucky breaks if you don't prepare the ground for the seeds to germinate in. Opportunities are all around us, all the time. Even my friend appreciates that, and he is actually quite astute in spotting them. He just won't take the plunge and follow through. Again, like a lot of people, he procrastinates – keeps putting things off – because grasping at opportunity is challenging. I suspect he feels safer remaining in his comfort zone (or rut, as I call it!)

If you spot an opportunity and don't seize it, someone else who is more open-minded and has more ambition and drive will step in. How many times have you seen something on television and remembered that you had that idea? They may fail to develop it fully, but they will at least try. And if they do make a success of that opportunity, it certainly won't be down to 'luck'. It will be thanks to optimism and enthusiasm.

Being lucky isn't about having some magic gene. It's not one of those 'some of us are born with it and some aren't' situations. Sure, there are times when something really fortunate *does* just happen out of the blue. But you don't win the football pools unless you send in your coupon. You don't get the promotion you really want unless you've prepared the ground with a load of hard work or, possibly, lots of intensive lobbying and getting to know all the right people (that can be hard work, too!) And you don't get to go out with a guy or girl you fancy unless you put yourself in the right place at the right time and actually ask them.

'Luck', as most of us understand it, does not exist in a vacuum (whoever heard of a lucky Dyson?) Luck happens because someone has created the perfect environment in which it can flourish. Even occurrences that, at first sight, seem to be pure chance need that fertile ground in which to take root. Another guy I knew would always put the minimum stake in every fruit machine he came across in a pub. The first time I saw him slip 10p in one – and win £50 – I thought he was a lucky so-and-so … until I realised that he had been doing the same thing for 10 years!

Luck – or the lack of it – can only come about after our approach to life has been determined: it simply doesn't come first. What it all boils down to is the truism that 'you've got to be in it to win it'. There is no shortcut to making yourself luckier, but at least the solutions are clear and simple, however trite the following statements might sound: 'Strike while the iron is hot'; 'Never put off until tomorrow what you can do today.'

Try and think first and foremost about what you *can* do in any given situation, not about what you can't. Be positive and optimistic in your outlook – not recklessly so – but optimism tempered with common sense is a sure-fire recipe for vastly improved luck. You must also be determined and tenacious because you never know when a door is about to open. Think of the vacuum-sealed jam jar that nobody can open: everyone tries but gives up in defeat, until a little girl comes along and, with one quick twist, pops the lid off. Luck like that is waiting to happen in countless places, but unless you make sure you're there at the right time, none of it will come your way.

Prepare for Success

When you start thinking about it, what others see as 'luck' is actually your reward. So what you have got to do is learn to put yourself in positions and situations that present you with the possibility of really good outcomes. When you're content to plod along, somewhere deep inside your own comfort zone, all you are really doing is trying to ensure that nothing bad will happen. How negative and defensive is that?

Think about your situation at work. Perhaps you feel that no matter how much effort you put in, you're never going to progress beyond a certain point. Maybe the sort of job you want simply doesn't exist in the organisation. The negative, 'unlucky' thing to do would be just to do the minimum amount of work to keep your job, and to stop those around you from thinking of you as 'work-shy'; always doing just enough, but never leaving your comfort zone, never pushing yourself or going the extra mile ... because it's just not worth the extra effort.

The thing is, you never know when a new opportunity might arise. Suppose the sort of job you ideally want is suddenly created – out of nothing – by a set of unusual circumstances. Imagine that there are two of you in your department doing pretty much the same thing. You have been ploughing your boring little 'do just enough' furrow, while your colleague – full of the enthusiasm and *naïveté* of youth – has been working her fingers to the bone. Managers have dumped extra work on her, knowing that she will tackle it ... and knowing that it's a waste of time asking you! There you are, chalk and cheese, when amazingly this opportunity arises – the one you have lusted after for years. What happens? You don't need to be a genius to work out who ends up being offered the promotion. 'Lucky so-and-so' you grumble quietly to yourself, and anyone in the pub who can be bothered to listen. Why didn't you get it? Because you didn't put yourself in a position to take advantage of what life throws at you!

Life isn't all about pigeon-holes. You should never assume that one thing can't leak into another, because it can. In the example above, you chose not to put in your best efforts because there was no immediate prospect of the reward you wanted. You pigeon-holed working hard in that particular job with there not being any immediate prospect of the promotion you wanted. But the two concepts refused to stay in the same pigeon-hole! Your hard-working colleague caught the boss's eye ... and then circumstances changed.

What Goes Around ...

There's a lot of truth in that old saying 'what goes around comes around'. You might not reap a reward tied specifically to the job you are currently doing. Your reward might come later – maybe even years later. Take the case of a friend of mine who was an advertising copywriter.

To start with, he loved the job, writing the adverts. As time went on, though, it became clear to him that all the copywriters were needed for was to churn out 'acceptable' copy for clients who really had no desire to pay for any sort of a 'deluxe' service. Nothing too fancy would do just fine, as long as it ended up sounding like a run-of-the-mill advert. When he started, he was even told by senior colleagues not to bother trying to be too creative, but simply to look back into the files of old ads and recycle the ideas. 'No one will remember – no one will notice anyway.' To his credit, he never actually did that (or so he assures me!) but, instead, tried to come up with a new idea for each brief he was given by the sales team.

It was hard work for little reward. In fact, people couldn't quite understand his keenness – even his boss! As time passed, though, even my friend was getting disillusioned. He really wanted to do more. He reckoned he could generate loads more business by going out and visiting clients with the sales staff. He even proved it on several occasions. But the story he got back – straight from the horse's mouth (the boss) – was that they couldn't afford to pay anyone extra to do this, and didn't really want to bother, anyway. So there was no prospect of promotion, just a fairly secure future manning the sausage machine.

At this, he could – very easily – have settled into the rut of doing just enough, of recycling all those old ads. But then, one day, a client came along who wanted to spend more money. They wanted 'an award-winning advert, no expense spared'. Aware that all expenses would be spared as far as he was concerned – even if he delivered the goods – he nevertheless rose to the challenge. Fortunately, he had kept on trying to think creatively even while churning out all those hundreds of potboiler adverts, and his mind was still quite fertile. Amazingly, he came up with an idea that not only won a big award in London, but also stuck in readers' minds for many years to come.

Although he had worked wonders, achieving everything and more that had been asked of him, there was still no reward. No promotion, just the same old, same old. The next year he wrote another advert – this time for a normal client who hadn't requested, or paid for, anything special – and that also won the top prize in London.

To cut a long story short, my friend never got a promotion. So eventually he moved on, going to work for the first company for which he had won an award. This would actually prove to be his first reward, and it only revealed itself after nearly three years, but even that didn't last long. Soon he had set up in business as a freelance writer. He got in touch with an old client he knew vaguely, wondering if he might be able to do any writing. Such was the impression he had created looking after that client's 'bog standard' adverts – and by subsequently writing his two award-winning adverts – that he was welcomed with open arms. He was given more work than he knew how to handle, and his business got off to a flying start – reward number two: delayed, but nonetheless appreciated. Some might say he was lucky, some said … but we knew better.

Even when there seems little chance of immediate reward, someone, somewhere will notice your efforts, talents or kindnesses. They will file them away for later, maybe when they can do something practical about it. It is always worth showing yourself in your best light. Do that, and you will deserve every little bit of luck that comes your way ... because you will have earned it!

Go on – give yourself a chance. Be lucky tomorrow!

TED'S STORY

The man who produced Radio Riverside's commercials would often shake his head in gloomy acceptance that life was destined never to be kind to him. In truth, he wasn't a gloomy person all of the time. It's just that bad luck seemed to follow him through life like some sort of vigilante rain cloud. Over the loudspeaker on the wall above his desk, Ted Wogan had just heard the news that half a dozen shop girls had won £2.5m each in the National Lottery.

As he continued with his tedious paperwork, a scriptwriter popped his head around the door. Asking if Neil had heard that last news report, Ted grumbled on about luck, asking why a bunch of shop girls could possibly need millions of pounds, and forecasting that it would only make them miserable. Mildly irritated by Ted's constant misery, Neil started to say that if Ted ever actually bought a ticket himself ... but was swiftly interrupted. 'What's the point? Someone else'll just go and win anyway – they always do. Life's a bitch and then you die.'

Rolling his eyes up towards the ceiling, Neil wondered aloud whether it might just be down to Ted's attitude. Ted had quickly, firmly and gloomily rejected this possibility. How could it be down to him that his wife walked off with the window cleaner? Or that some bastard scratched his car last week in the multi-storey? Or that he was stuck in some Mickey Mouse job when he could have been running his own radio station in Manchester? That, apparently, wasn't down to Ted – it was just the luck of the draw.

Ted did seem to have had more than his fair share of life's crap heaped upon him – but people sort of expected it to happen now. It was in his make-up. True, he had once been offered the chance to run a radio station himself, but he'd turned it down for something he thought was safer and, perhaps, less of a personal challenge. Promises made to him had evaporated into the mists of time, and he had been left – once again – cursing his misfortune. When Ted talked like this, it was hard to believe that this was one of the most talented, conscientious and decent people you could ever hope to meet. Someone who – although he refused to believe it – was rated at the top of the heap by everyone whose professional path he had ever crossed. Ted just expected bad things to happen – indeed, he was almost relieved when they did. It proved his judgement correct.

When Neil returned from his 'fag break', Phil, the other scriptwriter in the office, turned the conversation to the weekend's big golf tournament on television. Both writers played the game. Ted, however, detested sport – presumably because it was competitive, and he was always destined to lose. The ensuing conversation revolved around the top golfer Tiger Woods – especially about one amazing stroke he had played. It had enabled him to complete a hole in just two shots – three less than its 'par' of five. Phil referred to this as an 'albatross' but Neil insisted it should be called a 'double-eagle', an American expression.

None of these ridiculous technicalities meant a thing to Ted, but he did have strong views on luck. He reckoned that nobody could deliberately hit a tiny white ball into a hole the size of his coffee cup 600 yards away. Out of doors, in the wind, on bouncy ground. In two shots!

Pure luck, Ted insisted, adding that Tiger's luck had probably won him a million dollars – something that would never happen to him. The two writers had turned on Ted, fiercely defending the virtues of hard work, practise, natural ability and having the right attitude. Neil added that, in any case, Ted would never know because he'd never give fate the chance to smile on him!

As usual in these exchanges, there was a point at which Neil – who was not, fundamentally, a particularly nice or sympathetic person – got totally exasperated with Ted's attitude. This time, he told him to stop whingeing and to do something positive, adding that he should have bought a Lottery ticket himself and, anyway, that he was already a whole lot luckier than 'the starving millions in Ethiopia'. Ted quickly agreed that they were definitely a bit unluckier than him.

Amazingly, in a fit of reckless optimism a few years ago, Ted had actually entered the Lottery for three weeks. He'd chosen the same numbers each time. In fact, everyone in the office knew those numbers off by heart – all birthdays. They'd jokingly take tickets out themselves using the same numbers, just to wind Ted up – it was the talking point of the department for a while! After three unsuccessful weeks, he'd got fed up – convinced he was never going to win.

During this current conversation, Neil had been looking at the morning paper as he'd railed at Ted. His eye caught the winning Lottery numbers and he began to read them out: '3 … 9 … 15 … 22 … 29 …'

Irritated, Ted indicated that yes, he'd got the message. He knew that they knew his numbers, but he had better things to do than sit there, listening to Neil being childish. He announced that he was going up to the studio to do some proper work, 'Away from you heartless bastards.'

But Neil hadn't finished. 'No Ted, seriously: 3 … 9 … 15 … 22 … 29 …

and what was the last one again? 31?' With that, Ted disappeared, oblivious to the fact that Neil had actually been reading the numbers from the newspaper. An hour or so later, Ted returned to find Neil still harping on about his numbers. 'By the way, Ted,' he continued, 'you know those shop girls? Well, they had your numbers, mate!'

Ted assumed that this was another stupid 'wind-up' until, that is, Neil showed him the paper. Ted bowed his head and held it in his hands for what seemed like an age. 'The bastards! They used my numbers! That's theft.' Unsympathetically, Neil said that it wasn't. It was, rather, simply a case of people making their own luck.

A few months later, after Ted had retired, Phil was watching television one night. It was the quiz show *Who Wants to be a Millionaire?* To say that he watched 'open-mouthed' would be an understatement: Ted was one of the contestants! Not surprisingly, he'd been on the verge of taking his cheque after only four questions. He'd 'ummed and aahed' extensively – and rambled on about how he was never lucky – but, somehow, had struggled through to £125,000. He'd used all his 'lifelines' bar one, and he really wasn't sure about tackling the £250,000 question. With a very un-Ted-like rush of blood, he'd decided to 'phone a friend'.

'Okay Neil, the next voice you're going to hear will be your ex-boss, Ted. He's doing pretty well, but he needs you to help him up to *a quarter of a million pounds.*'

Neil! Jeez, Phil had thought, that was some risk. After all, Neil had never even turned up to Ted's leaving do. They'd fallen out after Neil had, once again, slammed Ted's negative attitudes.

'Hi Neil ... In British golf, a score of three under par is: A – a super-eagle? B – an albatross? C – a triple-birdie? Or D – a double-eagle? Come on mate – I'm relying on you!'

Less than graciously, Neil answered that it was D – a double-eagle, and that – yes – he was certain. Ted thanked him, but had not looked happy. The game show host then asked Ted if he was going to go with his friend's confident answer. Ted agreed that he'd sounded confident, but that he wasn't at all sure, saying that all he really knew about golf was that it was about luck. 'Sod it,' he said, recklessly, and plumped for answer 'B'. It was to be his absolute and final answer: 'B – an albatross.'

Phil thought Ted was right, but the wait seemed to go on for ever. Neil and he had argued in the office about it once – months earlier – while Ted was having an extended whinge. Phil further recalled that they'd never actually agreed on their final answer. Anyway, after another ad-break, there it was: answer 'B', up in lights! Ted had made a decision! Best of all, he got the next one right, too. Okay, he cashed in his money on half a million, but he'd finally got lucky. And he claimed not to have had a clue where the inspiration to contradict his friend came from. Said that it was just ... Lady Luck, smiling on him. Ted had, at last, bought his ticket, and he'd won his lottery. And about time ...

Ted's Experience

Luck is not an intangible subject. It is very real and something we have control over. Luck is chiefly governed by attitude. Accidents only happen in threes because we expect them to. We are 'human magnets' and attract people and circumstances according to our outlook. Do depressed people hang out with depressed people? Do successful people know successful people? And does money go to money?

Think about your lucky break and analyse what hand you had in it. I bet you made it happen by making the appropriate decisions; it wasn't the invisible hand of fate.

Who are the luckiest people you know? What are their personalities, and how might they bring this upon themselves?

Be Persistent

Persistence is an odd thing. How would you behave if you were persistent? Think about some successful people – either people you know or people in the public eye. How do they exhibit persistence? How do they make their luck? Really build a picture of what you would do differently if you had that ethic.

Choose one thing out of the various answers you come up with and do it tomorrow. Break it down into its component parts and start to be it, bit by bit. If you can do it for a whole week, that would be even better – but no pressure, eh?

Points to Remember

- **Expectation often becomes reality.** Think good thoughts as they will become your actions.

- **We are all influenced.** That's not a bad thing if our influences are positive.
- **Opportunities are often discovered by optimism!**

CHAPTER 10

Don't Expect too Much of Others

THIS MIGHT SOUND a touch cynical, but it's true: there's only one person whose behaviour you can control 100 per cent. That's you. Everyone else has it in them to surprise you by reacting in a way you never thought they would – even your mother! And because people can surprise you, they can throw you off course, sometimes to a considerable degree.

Friendship and Trust

Imagine, for instance, you have been friends with someone for years. Good friends. A trust has built up whereby you can say virtually anything to each other without serious offence being taken. Then imagine it all going pear-shaped!

If you look around your own good friends, you might find this difficult to picture, because the longer people are friends, the stronger is the bond that becomes established. What happens with a friendship is that you generally grow to accept the other person, 'warts and all'. Nobody is perfect – we all have failings, bad habits, irritating tendencies. But a good friend will take the entire package and accept that your good points will considerably outweigh your weaker ones. On balance, that makes you a solid friend and, to complete the friendship, you do the same. You accept your friend's shortcomings, appreciating that we all have them.

You will probably ignore such faults altogether to begin with – indeed you might not even see them at all. But, after a while, as you really get to know someone well, their failings will become apparent ... as will yours. So what do you do? How do you both react?

As I see it, a good friend will know that sufficient trust exists between the two of you to enable either of you to be prepared to accept constructive criticism. Indeed, many people think that part of being a really good friend to somebody involves some sort of obligation to help them see where they might be going wrong. A true friend should be able to hold up a pure, non-distorting mirror that can help you rectify any flaws before they become serious enough to cause more general problems in your life. I'm not saying that they should stick that mirror right in your face all the time, or preach at you incessantly, but you should certainly be aware that you are being monitored in a quietly supportive way. In this way, a friend should be able to help you to help yourself.

However, because we are all human beings with desires, ambitions and emotions – and not computers ruled simply by pure logic – things can go awry. Personal or business relationships can be put under strain, even pushed to the limit. External forces can twist our thinking – we can become irrational – and that's when relationships can shatter.

This is never pleasant, but it is the aftermath that's usually the worst part. You have invested a lot of trust in someone else. You've shared secrets, made yourself vulnerable. Should that trust be violated, there is a great danger that your instinctive reaction will be one of never trusting again. When a love affair implodes, you might be left brokenhearted, and so painful do you find it all that you swear you will never love again. Never again put yourself in a position of such vulnerability. Half the pop songs in the history of the world were written with just this scenario in mind!

It's very likely that, if you're a sensitive, thinking person, you'll turn things round on yourself and question your own judgement. 'How come I never saw that coming – it must have been so obvious!' Depending on how hard you get hit by any break-up, that questioning of judgement might spill over into life outside the friendship – to such a point that you completely lose faith in your ability to make decisions. It affects your self-esteem, becomes a major obstruction in future personal relationships as your baggage travels with you, and can have serious implications for your professional career. This is because, as we have already talked about, confidence is key to a happy and successful life.

Analyse Your Friendships

Make a list of your friends. Now make a list of the things you like about them. Which traits do you like in them that other people might not? Do you have two friends who don't get on? If so, what are the traits that allow that to happen (not the incidents or events; we're talking personality)?

Be Realistic

So how do we retain our ability to strike up meaningful friendships without putting ourselves potentially in the way of such risks again? It's a balancing act that's as delicate as the inside of a complex watch mechanism, yet the real secret is actually surprisingly easy to put into action. What you have to do is simply accept that things will go wrong in life (we already looked at this inevitability when we agreed that 'shit happens', earlier in this book), but that rarely is it entirely your fault. If a relationship breaks up, there will be fault – or, at the very least, elements of incompatibility – on both sides. If a relationship is meant to last, it will. Equally, if it is not meant to last it will have a finite lifespan. As long as you are realistic enough to appreciate that, sometimes, things don't work out, you'll be okay when you reach that point.

So the answer is that you must be prepared to give away some of your trust. By doing this you will be able to establish those friendships and relationships that can generate so many good things, and make us so happy and fulfilled. However, you don't need to give away every last bit of your trust. You must retain enough so that you can stand on your own two feet as and when you need to. You must never lose sight of the fact that even your best friends can let you down. Hopefully, they won't, but they can. If they do, the disappointment shouldn't dent your confidence too deeply.

You can always hope for perfection in others, but you should never expect it! For some of us it's the same when someone close to us dies. Because we have, perhaps, invested too heavily in someone else, we can feel horribly let down when this happens. But if we can accept mortality, we can cope with it and, gradually, start building our life up again.

Just as we shouldn't expect immortality from anyone, we shouldn't bank everything on another's generosity, dependability, honour, devotion or loyalty. We must understand that even strong people can have moments of weakness and, when they do, that such moments can collapse our house of cards.

All a bit serious, perhaps, but it really does boil down to one thing: be ready to rely on yourself just in case other people – whether in your business or your personal life – let you down. You're right to demand plenty and expect a lot of other people, but accept that this may not be how it is from time to time.

Learn to Deal with Your Emotions

There are many things we blame for holding us back in life. However, the truth is that it will only ever be our own thoughts holding us back. We have all gone through different journeys in our life, from our childhood to this very day. Take a moment or two to allow some experiences to spring to mind now. You may recall some of these as unpleasant, while others will be enjoyable and make you smile. But they are all relative to us as individuals.

Although we cannot change the experience, we can forgive the emotion we attach to it. For example, as a six-year-old child, you had every right to be scared of your bullying mother. You were a young, vulnerable child without the skills to deal with this situation – but why should your mother have that hold on you now, as an adult? The child and the adult are completely different people, and as an adult you have all the wisdom, knowledge and expertise to deal with this situation in the right way.

As a child you could not control another person's thoughts and actions. And still, as an adult, you cannot control someone else, so how do you stop feeling trapped or bullied? You have the choice of how you want to deal with any situation that comes your way. By choosing not to feel those negative thoughts that were always attached to a situation or person (in this case your mother), you are taking yourself out of that circle and deciding to think differently about it. The same applies to your relationships. Instead of spending your days fighting to change how another thinks and deals with their life, just accept them as their own person and choose to change the relationship that you have with them. So, instead of feeling constantly let down by, say, your mother in the way that she speaks to you or treats you, just change the way that you see your relationship.

If your mother doesn't fit the profile that you would like her to, don't try to mould her to it; just accept her for who she is and create a new, realistic profile for her. You have freedom and choice to think and feel what you like, just as she does. Creating harmony isn't a matter of everyone thinking the same way; it is through our acceptance that we will change the situation.

THE STORY OF GERRY AND MEL

'Just a quiet word of warning, Gerry. It might be an idea to keep an eye on your mate Mel.'

Brian and Gerry were part of a sizeable group of regular Sunday-morning pub footballers, most of whom had just finished playing – or watching – a feisty cup tie, and were cheerfully 'rehydrating' in the public bar. Brian – no stranger to the art of political manipulation within the group – had eased Gerry to one side in order to impart this somewhat cryptic warning. On this occasion, however, Gerry sensed that the comment was made not out of a desire to 'stir the pot' but, genuinely, with the best of intentions.

'Why – what's he done?'

'It's what he's been saying out there ... about you. Have you two had a falling out lately?'

'No, at least I'm not aware of it if we have! What do you mean?'

Gerry and Mel had been friends for a good many years. They'd met up through playing football against each other, then Mel had moved house and decided to join Gerry's club. They got on well – had similar tastes in music, similar views on the world at large and both enjoyed a pint. When the bruises and strains started taking longer to heal and the time came to hang up the boots, both felt that competitive sport was still essential to life, and chose to stay in touch with the game through coaching and management. Eventually they ended up at this pub, where they seemed to come as a ready-made pair and were obviously longstanding friends. They played as a team in darts competitions; obviously, they drank with each other; and their families even holidayed together. To say that Brian's warning intrigued Gerry would be an understatement; he was baffled, and keen to discover more.

'Well, to be honest, he didn't sound very much like a friend today. Every time your name came up he had something critical to say. Like how "tight" you are – according to him – and how difficult you are to socialise with nowadays. And how boring you are because you won't try and drink him under the table any more. I must say it surprised me – as far as I've seen, you've always paid your way. None of us lot has any problem with you. And he drinks like an idiot anyway – must cost him a fortune! Anyway, just thought I'd let you know, as it was a tad embarrassing.'

'Well, yeah, it would be. Sorry for that. You've got me there. It just doesn't sound like him. Not the sort of thing he'd do. I believe what you say, but I don't know what he's on about.'

Gerry was genuinely puzzled. Sure, there were things about each of them that would occasionally irritate the other. Mel would brag about being handy with his fists and 'sorting people out', although Gerry had never been close to witnessing any such behaviour from him. He presumed these tales to be a fantasy designed to create some sort of tough-guy image, for whatever reason. What was certain was that none of their mutual friends were ever present at these incidents, and they always seemed to happen hundreds of miles away! Then there was his penchant for making entirely predictable but harmless racist comments: meant to be amusing and said without malice, they could nonetheless offend people. Or those embarrassing, over-the-top displays of apparent generosity, like insisting on buying pints for 25 people when everyone concerned would have been far more comfortable drinking in small groups. All of these were the sort of minor faults that friends put up with: Gerry did, anyway.

Likewise, Mel put up with what he saw as Gerry's meanness (maybe because he would never buy drinks for 25 people all at once!) and his reluctance to drive anywhere. Mel used to assume that it was because Gerry wanted to enjoy a few pints, but wouldn't drink and drive. Mel would, and ended up as a perpetual chauffeur. Later he realised that drink had very little to do with it – Gerry just hated driving – but this still occasionally rankled with him, even though Gerry always repaid him in some way or other. Gerry's surreal sense of humour would clash with Mel's more basic 'Benny Hill' appreciation of comedy, and Gerry appeared reluctant to either take, or give, advice about sport, while Mel seemed to want to do both.

All in all, both saw each other's good points as outweighing the bad, and 'mateship' – rather than friendship – flourished. But what Gerry had just heard upset him, and he resolved to straighten Mel out. His way was always to confront these things head on, as he detested going behind people's backs. He arranged to meet Mel for a pint later that week. When he put Brian's information to him (without naming his sources, naturally), Mel was evasive, pretending to be unaware of it all. Gerry made it clear that they were still mates and, as such, if anything needed saying it should be done face to face – no offence would be taken. Sheepishly Mel agreed, and that was everything sorted out – apparently. Gerry, however, was still at a loss to understand what he saw as a good mate's unexpected disloyalty.

Over the next few weeks, it became clear to everyone who knew him that Mel seemed to be getting unusually 'matey' with Adrian, an unpleasant, manipulative, self-important little man who rather fancied himself as the football club's 'king-maker'. Gerry had little time or respect for Adrian's pomposity, and Adrian, in turn, was utterly clueless as to how to handle Gerry's dry wit. But so much did Mel now seem to fawn all over Adrian that he was compared – unfavourably – to a young puppy frantically collecting any stick that might be thrown for him.

All of this coincided with Mel's elevation at work from jobbing plumber to the grandly titled role of 'Operations Manager' (for which he had a brass plate made to screw to his new office door). This equivalent of 'getting the key to the executive toilet' seemed to be going to his head. It was also rumoured that Adrian was actively encouraging Mel to stand for a committee position. Playing on Mel's own newly found self-importance, he rather enjoyed having a tame sidekick pandering to his every need. Gerry, meanwhile, was observing all this with mild disappointment. Mild, at any rate, until the next incident ...

For several months, Gerry had been secretly planning – with Mel's wife – a surprise 40th birthday party for Mel. The cover for this was that Gerry, with his own wife, would be treating all four to a slap-up dinner in town by way of celebration, but they would actually all end up at a hotel function room where the secret party was to be held. This had been 'arranged' for months, but then Mel dropped his bombshell. As Gerry passed a table in the bar where Mel was drinking with Adrian, he quietly reminded him of the meal, which was only a week away. In a very off-handed way, Mel answered: 'Oh, sorry mate, can't make it after all. I've an important meeting with Adrian at the Conservative Club. Can't be helped – one of those things. Another time, maybe.'

They had clearly been drinking together for a while, and both seemed to find Gerry's irritated response mildly amusing: 'Oh, for good-ness' sake. You've known about this for ages, Melvin! I'm sure one little meeting isn't going to change the world.'

'You clearly don't know how important this could be for me. There could be high office at stake.'

'Right! So you'll be arse-licking at the Con Club, then, rather than sharing one of life's pivotal moments with good friends?'

'Gerry, go away. If you don't realise how much kudos my new job carries, that's your problem.'

Quietly seething, Gerry left the table. When, an hour or so – and several whiskies – later, Gerry bumped into Mel in the gents, he decided to give it both barrels. He pointed out just how silly he was making himself look to everyone else, being Adrian's lapdog. He told him that friendships were more important than so-called social status. And when this cut no ice, Gerry told him that he was being a complete arse with no sense of loyalty whatsoever. Mel thereupon very publicly 'took the hump'.

When they returned to the bar, Mel told all and sundry how let down he had been by his so-called friend, and how Gerry's insults to him were 'unforgivable'. The fact that Gerry was nearby, and already admitting that he had passed on a few robust home truths, made it appear that maybe he – rather than Mel – was at fault. What Gerry couldn't let on, though, was that a surprise party had been planned. In the background, Adrian could be spotted smirking to himself.

'It'll all be over by Christmas – these spats between friends always are,' Brian reassured Gerry the next weekend. But Mel seemed in no mood to mend any fences. In fact, he got into a more and more high-profile sulk with his one-time friend – one which lasted nearly 10 years, during which time Mel got on to the football committee, became chairman, and had a new brass plate made for the front door of his house to celebrate his lofty social status.

Although accepting the reality of this bizarre situation, Gerry was still unable to comprehend that something he'd done had so comprehensively unbalanced their relationship. He never understood how Mel could have changed his personality so significantly and so quickly. He was genuinely upset to watch his transformation from 'salt of the earth' to pompous buffoon, and to see how others had grown to detest him. All Gerry had ever expected from Mel was that he would be loyal enough to excuse a few relatively minor flaws in return for him doing the same, and that they would share a pleasant friendship for a long time to come. The surprise party was, of course, cancelled and Mel never discovered that he had missed out on this wonderful gesture from his friends.

It was many more years before he was told, on excellent authority, that Mel had actually engineered their final disagreement (having failed with his first attempt). Nothing Gerry could have done would have had any effect, it seemed, once Adrian had advised Mel that 'ditching the loose cannon' (that was how Adrian viewed Gerry) would be his passport to committee and beyond. Gerry heard this straight from the horse's mouth – from Adrian himself after he, too, had eventually outlived his usefulness. So good was Mel at long-term planning, developing useful friendships and then forcing their disintegration that few could ever see through the pretence.

Gerry became philosophical about it all. It was a shame, and annoying that he was taken in, but it taught him a valuable lesson about people. The next time a friend let him down badly (and it did happen), he wasn't that surprised and it didn't upset him as much. 'You just can't always take everything at face value,' he thought. Or, as his mum used to say, 'There's nowt so queer as folk, especially live ones.'

Gerry's Experience

First and foremost, Gerry's story is about expecting someone else to behave as he would to them, and being disappointed when this didn't happen.

Having known his friend Mel for years, he had worked on the assumption that he knew him really well, that he could depend upon him and that he could trust him, come what may. But what he failed to allow for was the fact that people change, for all sorts of reasons.

In Mel's case it was suddenly realising that he could attain what he saw as a significant jump in his social status. It had never really bothered him before but, as with so many people of his age, there was an element of mid-life crisis about it all. It was almost a case of 'now or never' and, to Gerry's huge disappointment, Mel's selfish pursuit of status was incompatible with their continuing friendship. To achieve this promotion, Mel had to sacrifice his relationship with Gerry, which he did.

The thing that we must all remember is that we can never be absolutely certain what other people might do, because their actions are out of our control. All that we can control is our own actions. It therefore follows that we should never expect things that are out of our control to be guaranteed: they might just change and upset our plans. So we must try not to be too disillusioned if that should happen. That's life. If we can make sure that such things don't totally surprise us, they can't hurt us too badly.

As Gerry discovered, it was unpleasant at the time but it taught him to be much more philosophical in the future. He would not be exactly cynical about friendships or relation-ships (social or business), just realistic. If they were solid and stayed that way, fantastic. But if things were to go pear-shaped, he would be in a mentally stronger position than before to accept it and get on with his life.

Developing Some of Your Characteristics

By understanding the way in which we communicate and relate to others, and the dynamics by which we interact, we can learn a lot about ourselves. As an exercise, think about the characteristics you would want to develop in order to socialise or get on in different circles. Have some fun with this.

Family Relationships

'Family' is a word with many different meanings and perceptions. We all know about the Waltons but does such a family exist? In my experience, the subject of family often brings with it words such as 'should', 'must' and 'obligation'. Some people may define the family as people who are related to us by blood or marriage. Others may believe family to be those we care for deeply and whose lives we share in. Ultimately, what's important is how we allow our relationships to be, within our family.

You must have heard the saying 'you can choose your friends but you can't choose your family'. But is family really about the people within your family or about the relationship you choose to have with them?

Let me explain. As we all know, everyone is different. It is only when we allow our 'family members' to be themselves and vice versa that we can obtain harmony. There are so many preconceived ideas of how a brother, sister, mother or father should be, but what happens when that person is not conforming to how someone wants them to behave? You can continually fight with them, but that does not make for a happy journey. Instead, by accepting that everyone is only human, including ourselves, we allow us all to make mistakes and learn from them.

Points to Remember

- **Trust does not take time.** Trust comes from honest and realistic evaluation.
- **Trust is a choice.** You choose to do it because it is worth having, but like anything worth having it carries risk.
- **Separate the incident from the emotion.** Any situation you were put in when you were young, you would probably have dealt with and felt differently about if it happened at any different stage. Forgive the emotional response the child gave to it. Imagine handling the situation with all the wisdom, knowledge and experience you have now. How different would it be?

Conclusion

Success is not a finite and tangible destination. It is a long and undulating journey. We are born imperfect, and will die that way. Therefore we are always in a state of learning. I would go as far as to say it is our main purpose on this planet. And as we discover more about ourselves, we find out more about others, enabling us actively to contribute to the world in which we live.

Index